UPFIELD
at
ALBERMARLE

Maxine Withers

Photographs by E.V.Whyte

ETT IMPRINT

Exile Bay

First published by ETT Imprint, Exile Bay in 2023

ETT IMPRINT
PO Box R1906

Royal Exchange NSW 1225 Australia

ISBN 978-1-922698-76-6 (hdbk)
ISBN 978-1-923205-97-0 (paper)
ISBN 978-1-922698-88-9 (ebook)
Ebook edition published 2024

Cover: The Hole family at Wheeler's Well, on Albermarle station, photographed by E.V. Whyte in 1923

Covers of Arthur Upfield's first editions courtesy Mark Terry at www.facsimiledusjackets.com

Designed by Tom Thompson

for
Verco Whyte

Arthur Upfield feeding a joey at Albermarle station, 1925.

CONTENTS

1 Upfield at Albermarle *7*

2 The Overseer *11*

3 Verco Whyte at Yalluna *21*

4 Albermarle *30*

5 Letters from the West *39*

6 Drought *55*

7 The Murchison Mystery *65*

8 Return to the East *75*

9 Sincerely Yours *90*

Notes *100*

Map of Albermarle *102*

Albermarle station, an oasis on the Darling River, photographed by EV Whyte from an enormous palm tree on the property, about 1920.

1.

UPFIELD AT ALBERMARLE

In the summer of 1922, Arthur Upfield was trudging along a rough, winding track beside the Darling River when he came to Albemarle Station fifteen miles north of Menindee. He pulled the swag off his shoulder, straightened his aching back and asked the manager for a job. The boss hesitated at first (there were already more than thirty men employed on the station), then he took pity on the tall, thin, dejected traveller and offered him some work repairing a fence. That job in the middle of summer nearly killed him, Upfield admitted in later years, but it was followed by easier work cooking for the men at the homestead and afterwards at a hut outback, where he was able to complete the first of his many books of crime fiction.

Upfield spent the greater part of five years at Albemarle, the longest period he had remained in one place since he arrived in Australia on 14th November 1911. He was born on 1st September 1890, the first-born son of a prosperous grocer of Gosport, on the western side of Portsmouth Harbour. There he spent a happy childhood with firm but indulgent parents, grandparents and aunts. An indifferent scholar in every subject except history and geography, he enjoyed reading and writing adventure stories and telling long, exciting tales to his four younger brothers. His interest in other times and distant places was stimulated by the fresh salt tang of the harbour, the ironclad ships and busy little steam ferries, the naval reviews at Spithead and Nelson's flagship *Victory*, which had prevailed against Napoleon Bonaparte and come to rest in moorings off Gosport. When he could not settle down to a tame career as an articled clerk in a firm of estate agents, auctioneers and surveyors, his father decided that he should go to Australia to learn farming.

It was not the seasonal routine of farming which appealed to the restless young emigrant. He wanted to go the bush. While working in and around Adelaide for several months he read Henry Lawson's short stories, Steele Rudd 's *On Our Selection* and the *Bulletin*, and scanned the Situations Vacant columns of *The Advertiser* for requests for a boundary rider. At last his persistent applications were successful and the firm of Elder, Smith and Company sent him to Momba, its large pastoral holding west of the Darling in New South Wales.

Arriving by train at Broken Hill in the early morning, he felt that he was at last in the real Australia. Horses were hitched to a rail outside the coach office at the Southern Cross Hotel, sun-tanned bushmen leaned against the verandah posts and a big coach was waiting in the yard. Wide verandahs screened with trailing vines still shelter the Southern Cross Hotel, but motel rooms, a swimming pool and parked cars now occupy the space which was the terminal for Morrison Brothers' four-horse coaches.

Arthur Upfield had arrived just in time. In December of 1911, his first year in the bush, a motor coach carried the mail from Broken Hill to Menindee, taking five and three-quarter hours for the seventy-mile trip, and the following year A.E. Pitts carted wool in his de Dion lorry and the first garage was opened in the Silver City. Upfield travelled to Wilcannia by coach with the celebrated driver Fred Essen handling the ribbons and stopping at horse changes and old wayside hotels such as Mount Gipps and Topar, which reminded the eager adventurer of wild west saloons. They travelled all day and all night, reaching Wilcannia at two o'clock the next afternoon after thirty hours on the track. At sundown he climbed on to a buckboard bound for Wanaaring on the Paroo. In the middle of the night he was delivered at Momba to begin his career as a roving station hand.

In August 1914, immediately after the outbreak of World War 1 he enlisted in the Australian Imperial Forces and served his adopted country at Gallipoli and in France, visiting his family on leave. He met and married Ann Douglas of the Australian Army Nursing Service and lived for a while in Melbourne when the war was over, but after the birth of their son Arthur in the early 1920's he escaped from domesticity and went back to the bush.

At Albemarle the manager, James Hole, and his overseer, Verco Whyte, had seen many cooks come and go, but never one with literary aspirations like Arthur Upfield. When they discovered that he was writing a novel and sending articles about Australia to English magazines, they encouraged his efforts, for everyone in the bush enjoyed reading, and books were swapped or borrowed until they fell apart. In 1924 after Upfield, in a manner more typical of station cooks, had fallen out with one of the hands and left Albemarle for a few months to work as a boundary rider on the dingo-proof fence bordering South Australia, Verco Whyte wrote to him and received the following reply:-

Dear Mr Whyte,
S.A .Border Fence,
c/o Quinyambie Station, via Tarrowangee, N.S.W.
6th September, 1924.

Your letter of August 16th to hand for which I thank you very much indeed.

I am delighted to hear that my string of oaths poetical and imbued with drama found such a grand echoe (sic.) in a swelling chorus at Albemarle...[1]

I suppose the excitement at Government House was intense when the Governor was there. Wish I had been cooking there then, would have given him the 'gutz-ache' for weeks, whilst as for Langwell - well, there would have been a new President of the Lands Board.

Many mistakes have I committed in my life and the greatest was in coming here - yea even greater than getting married. This Quinyambie is supposed to be a cattle station... During the three months I have been here I have been able to obtain meat three times. The price of rations is scandlous (sic.) - Baking Powder 3/-, tea 3d, sugar 10d, flour 6d. There are no dogs - no foxes. The camels are old and worn out. Everything has gone bung. I am very blue.

So I have written to Mr Hole asking if he will take me back into the fold. I am pining for a 'hunk' of mutton and a good drink of tea. Perhaps I might see you soon, perhaps - but do not let us despair.

My book continues to remain an Also Ran, but I am still hopeful. Lately I have engaged in answering the Agent General for South Australia who had the cheek to reply in criticism to some of my articles on Immigration appearing in a South of England paper. If the Editor of the paper has sufficient courage to publish my open letter to the A.G., the A .G. will have ten fits and throw two sevens. "The cow! I'll put it across him".

Please thank Sid for his letter enclosed with yours. Was highly amused re Vigar and Grow-Thin. You know, History repeats itself constantly. Was it not the Earl of Warwick who was dubbed 'The King Maker'? And now we have the soul of the Earl of Warwick reincarnated in Henry Vigar. Note the similarity of the ego. The Earl made and unmade English kings. Henry Vigar makes and unmakes Australian cooks. Vive Le Vigar! Vive the Cook-maker.

Please give my regards to your brother and Mr J. de C.

Hoping you are now free from the Dog Disease.

I am,

Yours sincerely,

Arthur W Upfield.

P.S. Keep this letter. Its value will be enormous when I am dead. Book lovers will buy up everything I have written. A.U.

He returned to the fold and the young overseer, taking his facetious instruction seriously, saved his letter and eventually had a collection of at least twenty-four, which described his efforts to earn a living with his pen.

2.

THE OVERSEER

Elson Verco Whyte had grown up on the land. He was born at Hawker, South Australia, in 1900, and when his mother died a week later he was reared by his widowed Aunt Frances at her farm three miles north of Minlaton on Yorke Peninsula.   His two sisters went to an uncle near Cleve until their father married again and then they returned to Angorichina Station which he managed for W.T. Mortlock of Martindale Hall, Mintaro. Years later 1n 1971 Verco Whyte wrote about bush life in the early part of the century:-

Towards the end of 1907 an upset occurred which probably had an effect on my whole life. Aunt Frances and I left Minlaton for Ango, for what I thought would be a holiday - a trip across Spencer Gulf in the steamer Karratta and then my first ride on a train. Dad met us at Parachilna and after dinner at the Hotel drove us to Ango where I met my sisters and Sid [born in 1904] for the first time.

After about a week for acclimatisation purposes 1 was "weaned". In spite of my protests and tears 1 was left behind when my aunt was driven off to catch the train and return to Minlaton. It was horrible and I don't like writing of it even now. I was impotent, though I tried to run after the buggy which was in sight for nearly a mile. I cried all day, but I suppose nature took over and I got over it to all intents and purposes. Aunt Frances later told me that she cried all the way down to Quorn on the way back and was an object of pity to others in the train. I suppose that incident helps to account for my soft-heartedness, which by the way should be called soft-headedness, and I don't like weaning calves or separating

Upfield's close friend, E.V. Whyte at Yalluna in 1918.

animals which have been running together and become attached to each other.

Life at Ango was different from at Minlaton. There the grocer called once a week after first coming for orders, and we would often drive into Minlaton for shopping on Saturday afternoons, besides the regular trips to Sunday School and frequent church services. Also we children saw neighbouring children fairly often even apart from meeting them at school.

At Ango groceries and most things came by donkey team and in large quantities; Jam by the case and flour by the 200 1b bag, sugar by the 70's, etc. Even the patent medicines were by the dozen or gross - Friars Balsam, Epsom Salts, Painkiller, Castor Oil (in those now valuable blue bottles), Aconite and other homeopathic medicines. Not only was there our family, but several blacks who in those days, before the dog fence was built about 1910, were engaged as shepherds. Each had at least one wife and one I remember had three. Dad was also issuing officer for government rations which were handed out to all the blacks. These included blankets and certain clothing, mostly piece lengths of cloth I think. I've an idea that Mum and Miss Pengelly [the governess]used to make them up into dresses, and I have vivid recollections of the manner the gins always wore their dresses, one arm through the armhole and the other through the opening with their neck, most becoming but uncomfortable. There were no other children to play with. Kate and Ruby were too old and being girls had nothing in common with me, and Sid was only three. We got a lot of enjoyment watching Dad when he was working about the place, particularly in the blacksmith shop which was the equivalent of the modern day workshop. School was held at regular hours in a pine and pug building which was part of the store and adjoined the shower room.

Camels at Upfield's Albermarle Station, 1920.

The tankstand (middle left) seen here with the Darling in flood about 1922.

Ango, which was near Blinman, had quite a big homestead of two storeys, but unfortunately it was burned down before Dad got there and the first thing he had to do was build a new house out of stone and mortar. It was not a thing of architectural beauty, but it was solid and cool in summer.

The Blinman copper mines closed down about the time of my arrival. There were two hotels, at least three shops and a doctor, Dr Lander. Although I didn't realise it I was witnessing the death of a mining town.   The three storekeepers were Williams, Jones and Nicholls who had a family of eleven children and were particular friends of ours. It was at their place I heard my first phonograph, with Edison-Bell records of wax cylinders. Nicholls went first. They bought a place up near Beltana, Warrioota or some name like that, and when we went up through Beltana in 1968 they still had it and Lance was running it. The other two stores battled on, supported by the few people left in the town and the surrounding grazing properties.

Some of the old hands were hopeful that the mine would re-open, but when the local school master bought the machinery and broke it up for scrap it was realised that the position was hopeless. The young chaps went first, and in some cases the mother and father stayed and kept the home going, living on their savings I suppose, as there were no pensions in those days. One way of making a few pounds in that area was "picking gum" from the wattle trees that grew on the hillsides. And there were always the rabbits. What part of Australia hasn't made money out of the bunny at some time or other?

We made our pocket money out of gum and rabbits. And it was all banked. The opportunities to spend it were few and far between. We used to get about 3d. per lb. for gum and 9d. per lb. for rabbit skins. There was no market for the carcases; about nine skins would go to the pound. Mum used to buy the gum from us and also from the blacks, and would send it away in wheat bags.

The stock did not water from troughs at Ango, nor from the ground tanks we are used to in the Darling country. All waters were in creeks, which were normally a chain of waterholes, running through only after rain. As the summer advanced the holes became smaller and smaller and some would go dry all together, but most creeks had a spring or two which needed cleaning out and assisting a bit. Then we would all be taken for a picnic - barbecues had not been invented. It was surprising what a few small boys and a couple of strong girls could do to help. Dad and the blackboys did most of it really, cleaning the spring out with a shovel and making a bank around to form a pond. It was our job was to collect a lot of stone as an edge to the pond. It was all very nice sweet water, no salinity problems. At the homestead was a well in the side of the creek which had a windmill to pump the water into a tank on the hill to supply the house and garden.

Jeff was born in 1908 (2 May to be exact) and Mum went to Port Augusta for the event. Dad took her to the train at Paralchilna and I went with him. It was a memorable trip. Dad had a pair of mules, Melba and Diana, that no one else was allowed to drive, in fact Melba had never even been handled by anyone else. They were champions, and I remember we finished the last five miles of the twenty-five in half an hour. We did not come straight back but called at Moolooloo twelve miles north of Angorichina and stayed the night. It was owned by Lindows, Mr, Mrs and Miss. They were shearing at the time and had a Chinaman cooking for the shearers, which intrigued me, especially when Mr Lindow told us about him. It appears that he was most upset one day because he had lost "him dishcloth" and pestered all and sundry, "Had they seen 'im." When he was dishing up the evening meal, he came into the dining room all beaming. "I find 'im, I find 'im!" "Where was it Charlie?" "In the cabbage", said Charlie happily.

We stopped two nights at Moolooloo, because the mules headed for home or somewhere and Dad had to borrow a horse and spend most of the day looking for them. The roads in the hills made it one of the last parts of the state to see motor vehicles. I remember when the first car came to Ange about 1910 with a party of government people, departmental or parliamentary, and they stopped the night with us, and what is more took us for our first ride in a car.

The first motor bike in the district might have been a little earlier. Mr P.A. Corry[2] the school master in Blinman bought one and got about the district quite well. It was modern enough to have a magneto in place of the dry cell for ignition. We had a nine-hole golf course and an earthen tennis court. Occasionally friends would come to play one or the other game and when Mr Corry got his motor bike it saved him a lot of pushing on his pushbike.

I don't remember the blackboys being particularly good at either tennis or golf, but they were good at throwing things and dodging them. I'm sure that cricket would have suited them much better. When playing with them I was allowed to throw sticks, stones, boomerangs, waddies or spears, provided I gave notice of intention, but I never managed to do any harm. I remember when out rabbitting one day getting a whack in the ribs with a spent boomerang which had been thrown end over end, and Tommy was most upset, thinking I might have been hurt. When rabbitting the blackboys would let the rabbit have a run for it. I was allowed to have a shot at them on the squat. We would walk miles after rabbits and Kate and Ruby could come too. We used waddies mostly and spent a lot of spare time in making them; I fear that we used a great deal of time which these days would be working time, but making those weapons, boomerangs, spears and waddies, was of much more interest to the black-boys than working, although they were prepared to work at any time they were needed, and I guess that they were not paid much in the way of wages.

Besides Ango, which was a hundred square miles, there was a lease of another one hundred square miles, Lake Tinko, out near Lake Frome. It was unimproved, but occasionally when there was good feed Dad would take a mob of sheep out there and leave someone with them.

In 1911 we left Ango and never returned as a family, though I did go back in 1916. I think that Dad thought he should take his family down into civilisation, where we would have a better chance of mixing with people, so when Mr Mortlock wrote and offered him the position of manager of Yalluna, near Tumby Bay on Eyre Peninsula, he decided to take it.

Moving was somewhat of a major operation. Mum, Ruby, Sid and Jeff went down to stay at Crystal Brook with the Youngs while Dad, Miss Pengelly, Kate and I with Blackboy Ted went via Port Augusta and from there overland to Rostrevor, Uncle Jim's place near Cleve. Miss Pengelly's family also lived at Cleve and she was able to stay with them. On the trip down from Port Augusta Dad drove four-in-hand in a buggy with back-to-back seating, two in front facing forward and two facing backward and sharing the same backrest. Teddy rode on horseback and was very useful in helping with the horses, and finding them each morning. Teddy and I learnt a lesson in Port Augusta. Feeling thirsty we went into the bar of a hotel to buy a lemonade. We were quickly hoisted out - he was black and I was much under age.

We stayed at Rostrevor for some time, over a month, perhaps two, and I learnt a lot about wheat cockying. I became great mates with my cousin Allan who was later killed in France. I used to "help" him with the wheat carting to Arno Bay where it was stacked until picked up by ketches, the small sailing vessel s which were the only size boats which could get into the Arno Bay Jetty. One lovely old draught horse called Noble was used to work the bag-lifter. He had to go forward perhaps ten yards until the bag was at the top of the wagon and when the bag fell off he turned round and went back again. I used to lead him and claimed that I was teaching him the routine. Everyone else said that Noble was teaching me.

We loaded up with wheat, perhaps eighty or more bags on a big tabletop wagon, in the afternoon of one day and got an early start next morning and took our lunch with us. I used to like it when we took bread and butter and bought a tin of sardines. We would eat them in the wagon coming home. There were eleven horses in the team: two in the shafts and three lots of three in the lead. There were reins on the shafters and on the outside leaders, the rest being only coupled together. I remember them bolting once as we started to come home.

Alan was not worried, there was no traffic to worry about and as he said, they will stop when they get tired. We were going the right way. Normally of course the pace was a walking one and sometimes Allan would get off and have a walk. The full distance there and back was twenty-four miles. Harnessing and unharnessing so many horses takes quite a lot of time, and eleven nosebags had to be carried to give them a bite while unloading was in progress - all manual - and the bags of wheat carried up on to the stack by "Jumpers". In the morning early the horses had to be fed and then when they got home in the evening and again before going to bed at night.

Another job I had was driving the horses in the chaffcutter. The horseworks consisted of a crown wheel driving a pinion on a shaft which in turn drove the chaffcutter. The chaffcutter was in the shed but the horseworks were outside. The horses were harnessed to a pole protruding from the crown wheel. They were coupled together and the inside rein was tied back to the pole so that they went round and round, but they needed someone to keep them moving. That was where I came in. Perched on a seat in the centre of the contraption I was given a whip to crack or even flip them with, but I had no means of stopping them. At several requests to "keep 'em moving" I got them a bit stirred up and they bolted. What consternation! All hands rushed outside and concentrated on giving me advice: "Don't jump Verco! Don't jump! Hang on! Hang on!"

Those were draught horses but they were galloping in the end, and fortunately the inside rein broke and they swung outwards and pulled the drawbar free from the pole. They galloped off with the swingle bars hanging and jumped the house paddock fence together like hunters. I wasn't allowed to drive the chaffcutter again. Lost my licence as it were. At Cleve I gamed my only experience "logging" with bullocks. This was done using two teams, one attached to each end of a heavy log in the form of a roller. It was cruder than those which pulled to one side of a single team, but equally effective. One team was always in the scrub and needed a good driver. The other walked over the fallen timber which was really no better. I was allowed to drive one team on rare occasions; just enough to say that I have worked a scrub roller drawn by bullocks. It was on the farm of Willie Whyte, Arthur Whyte's father, who had a farm adjoining Rostrevor, but later took up land at Kimba when that area was opened up.

Our family was united again when Mum and Ruby and Jeff travelled by train from Crystal Brook to Wallaroo and there caught the steamer to Arno Bay where, as the custom then was, it anchored out from the Jetty and we who had driven from Rostrevor and Cleve were rowed out and either climbed a ladder or were hoisted aboard in a basket. I think that I suffered the indignity of the latter. By breakfast time next morning we were in Tumby, where Dad was waiting to meet us with the buggy and four-in-hand.

Verco Whyte with two Aboriginal stockmen, at Ango Station.

3.

VERCO WHYTE AT YALLUNA

Now let us find out why we had proceeded in such a roundabout way from Angorichina to Yalluna. I didn' t find out until sometime later.

Mr Dutton was the manager of Yalluna. He was seventy years old and had been manager about forty years, so it was a bit of a shock when a complete stranger drove up in a four-in-hand accompanied by a black boy - there had been no blacks about there for twenty years - and announced that he was the new manager. Dad got a shock too, because he didn't know that Mr Dutton didn't know that he was coming. However, they got on well together. The Duttons shifted to a house at Poonindie, about seven miles from Port Lincoln, and with an old pony and phaeton for transport were happy in retirement and occasionally came back to Yalluna for a visit. They were a great couple, with many yarns of the early days, and she was always ready for a lark. One night she dressed up in men's clothes and "wanted to see the boss on business". She had us all taken in for a moment when she knocked on the door and made her request.

Tumby Bay, originally Tumbling Bay I've heard, is merely an indentation on the east coast of Eyre's Peninsula, but sheltered in some degree by a small island to the south, always referred to as "the island" and uninhabited. Although only about half a mile offshore, or perhaps a mile, distance at sea is deceptive, we never visited it. We were not a sea-going family I fear.

I suppose the population was about seven or eight hundred when we arrived. The chief industry was connected with Yalluna, or the station as it was usually called. The station carried 17,000 sheep. As well as the homestead at Yalluna with men's quarters' or half a dozen permanent hands, there was as outstation at Warratta twelve miles to the north with an overseer or offsider or two, according to the seasons. Over the hills and thirty miles in a direct line to the west was Coffin Bay with another two or three permanent hands and Mr Mortlock's summer house. Sheep were seldom run there but a hundred or so horses did. It was what was called "coastie" country, which meant that the sheep and horses got coast disease and had to be shifted on to different pastures. After we left there it was found that the trouble was a mineral deficiency, copper being the chief need, and I think that now the matter has been rectified. The wool of sheep would go steely and lack character, and horses would lose their manes and tails.

In any case it was very poor country with limestone near the surfaces and in places about it. I'm sure that it was valued more as a summer residence by Mr Mortlock, and it excelled at that. A solid stone residence right on the seashore surrounded by large pines and in those days the whole bay to himself. Only very rarely did a fishing party intrude as it was some miles off the road and the track a private one into the homestead.

In Tumby Bay there were two hotels, both two-storey buildings. The chief one belonged to Yalluna, or "Mortlock" as was usually stated. There were three stores and the principal one was Mortlock's, one bank, the building owned by Mortlock, a blacksmith shop, Mortlock's of course, and the butcher's shop. There were in addition at least a couple of dozen private houses, all Mortlock's. The hospital and doctor's residence were on Mortlock land which had been given to the hospital. The Church of England was in part a memorial to the Mortlock family and had stained glass windows proclaiming it. Tumby was a wheat farming centre and half the farms round about belonged to Mortlock. Part of Yalluna, they were used for grazing sheep when not under crop. Collecting rents was part of the job of management and an office was established in Tumby for the purpose. A station bookkeeper was appointed and set up in Tumby - in a Mortlock house of course - and he had one day set aside for rent collecting, but mostly came out to Yalluna for the day, on horseback or driving a jinker.

It was Saturday morning when we arrived and I can remember the thrill of it still. Fancy going to a new home with all sorts of new places to explore and investigate.

The house was large and solid with stone walls and slate roof, more rooms than we were used to, a nice flower and vegetable garden with a full-time gardener and a shade house for pot plants. Of course the homestead had kerosene lamps and no bathroom. For some time it was a case of bath in the very large kitchen in front of the fire with hot water from an enormous built-in copper, or have it in your bedroom.

The kitchen at Yalluna, in keeping with the custom of the time when it was built, late in the 19th century, was separate from the house and the poor domestics of the day had to carry the meals a good ten yards down a couple of steps and up again at the other end. In a fit of modernisation before we came the kitchen was connected to the dining room by a covered way on the same level - nearly - actually the dining room was lower so that the passage, as it was always called, had a definite slope in the floor towards the dining room. It was built of galvanised iron and did not harmonise with the rest of the building, but being at least eight feet wide it was a very handy adjunct for the ironing table, a cupboard and hanging space.

One hundred yards below the homestead were the buggy shed, stables, harness and saddle rooms, all of stone, and the haystacks. The five stalls housing the five stallions were separate but adjacent and being more modern were made of timber and iron. There were Clydesdale, Arab, Welsh, Shetland and Blood entires in the stalls and a Jack Donkey in the paddock. An engine room housed the old Ruston Hornsby engine for driving the chaffcutter (no horseworks here). The old straw-roofed shed, which we knew as a bough shed, was used to house the farming implements, drill, binder, wagon, etc.

Around the side of the hill about 300 yards away were the men's huts, another stone building of three rooms with the cook's quarters and kitchen nearby.

Here also were the poison rooms, three rooms housing poison carts, poison and various odds and ends. Lower down the hill and on the bank of a creek which usually ran a small stream were the woolshed, sheepyards and sheepdip. It was the first time we had seen a sheepdip and the last time I saw anything like it. You did not try to drive the sheep into the dip but forced them into a pen and pulled a lever and they all fell in.

One of the most interesting places of all was the blacksmith shop situated between the men's hut and the woolshed on the bank of the creek. Here in a primitive hut lived the gardener, "Old Prince", but to the junior members of the family, Mr Prince. We were not allowed to call any of the men by their Christian names unless they were young or had asked us to.

It was a pretty big day, that first day, and it was a long time before we were really well acquainted with our surroundings and the different type of living. The country was different. The winters were wetter. The sea was handy, but we did not use it much the first summer. Five miles was five miles in those days, especially when it was necessary to catch your transport and either saddle or harness it to a buggy. First of course it was necessary also to get permission to do either. We went to Sunday School each Sunday and usually to church also and in the summer we ran down along the beach or down the old jetty. The port of Tumby was not considered a busy one but it was always an attraction to me and I think all the family. Having lived so long inland any big supply of water, such as a river or lake, would have been an attraction, but when it was a port, well so much more romantic.

Each Wednesday and Saturday the sail boat would come in. On Wednesday it would arrive about 3 p.m. from Port Lincoln having come from Port Adelaide which it left twenty-four hours previously. On Saturday it arrived at the new jetty in the early morning, having been up the gulf in the meantime as far as Cowell and Wallaroo where it again

again picked up mail from Adelaide brought by train. The Adelaide Steamship Company ran the boats.

While these steamers ran to a timetable, quite a lot of cargo was carried in ketches, two-masted sailing ship, which used the old Jetty and were a common sight. The ships which created the greatest interest were the three-or even four-masted grain ships from overseas which came each year to load wheat. They would tie up at the Jetty and some could take on all their load before sailing away. Others that drew more water would have to go out perhaps half a mile and top up by means of a ketch.

All of these shipping movements could be seen from the front verandah at Yalluna, and many a time I've watched the big ships coming in to berth, using the old binoculars which Dad had brought with him from Ango where he used them for mustering in the hilly country. I remember watching one boat come in to berth and when we went to town the next day we found that as the sailors were taking in sail as they neared port, a young apprentice had fallen from the yardarm and crashed to his death on the steel deck.

At times there were brawls between the sailors and the locals, caused of course by drinking, and then the foreigner was a foreigner and not a new Australian. On one occasion there was quite an upset when Bill, the men's cook at Yalluna, got into an argument in one of the pubs and the sailor knifed him. He had to go to hospital for repairs, for he was stabbed in the stomach and as he himself said, "I had to hold my guts in with one hand till I got to the Doctor; and I know the colour of my caul fat, it's yellow".

A wheat ship in port was a source of employment for the locals. There was no such thing as bulk handling of the wheat cargoes. Each bag had to be lumped from the stack on to a rail truck which was hauled down the Jetty by horses and then again lumped off the truck on to a chute which ran into the hold of the ship.

Our trips to Coffin Bay, thirty miles away, were in the winter or "off" season when no other more important people needed it. My first trip down was with horse and buggy, and I can still remember how cold it was In the buggy which, though it had a hood to keep rain or sun off to a certain extent, never seemed to do anything to interfere with the wind, certainly not to warm it; and as usual my chief trouble would be my feet, and I was not alone. I remember that Dad sometimes let us boys out to have a run and warm our feet, but he being the driver had to suffer and stay put.

At Coffin Bay Mr Mortlock always had a yacht of some sort. We never used it, nor would we have expected to do so, as it was only used when Mr Mortlock was in residence. One of his favourite occupations was shark fishing and the West Coast, being on the ocean, is a good area for sharks. Another of "W.T.'s" hobbies was drinking whisky and we were fascinated to know that he drank a bottle a day and it was always good whisky and cost 7/6. As a comparison of wealth, I have always compared it in my mind with the 7/6 per week that my sisters Ruby and Kate were each paid for doing the housework. They had divided the work of Sophie Ahang (the former housemaid, of whom more anon) and also her salary.

There were occasions of course when W.T. had more then one bottle a day and there were some people who thought it might be a good idea to get him a bit bright before trying to do business with him. It never worked because he just would not talk business when he had had too much to drink. "No! We won 't talk about that, huh, huh", he would say. He nearly always finished his remarks with a couple of what I would call interrogatory "huh huhs". He used to come to Tumby by the usual passenger boat and Dad would meet him with a four-in-hand outfit and take him where he might want to go, but about 1912 apparently the roads and conditions were considered good enough to bring the car over. He had a chauffeur and his car was a big green Talbot. Mind you, he needed a driver-mechanic, because there were not many cars in those days and if anything went wrong there were no mechanics anywhere in the district.

And now to revert to Sophie Ahang. The Commonwealth census was taken just after Dad arrived and he had to ask information about Sophie. In reply to "What is your nationality?" Sophie thought that they had better put down "Comeback" and explained that her grandfather had been Chinese, her grandmother a black gin and her mother had married a Malay! She had a heart of gold and went to live with her widowed mother and I think two brothers.

Later she was to be a prodigious worker for the Red Cross in the 1914-18 War. Her brother Billy Ahang came back from England after the war with an English bride, and by a strange coincidence her name was Mortlock but not claiming any relationship with Yalluna Mortlock.

When I was about fourteen, it was decided that I should go per saddle pony to Tumby each day to the public school. At the beginning of 1915 I went to Adelaide to St Peters Collegiate School, commonly known as Saints ... Years later when Colin Matheson, who was a couple of years younger than I, came to Albermarle as a jackeroo, he reminded me that he had held my coat for me in the brawl with Princes (Prince Alfred College) at the intercollegiate school sports in 1915.

If I had to bring back anything of those "good old days", it would be the absence of fast traffic on the roads. There were so few cars that we knew the regulars not only by sight but by hearing, and there were all horse drawn delivery vans, carts, etc., and of course most city people travelled by trams.

There were not the great shortages that necessitated rationing in the second world war. As far as motor transport was concerned it was not really essential. Not many tractors would have been in Australia and I don't remember seeing any working on farms until after the war. In fact, riding to Adelaide from Albemarle in 1921, I was surprised to see tractors at work in the paddocks in South Australia and the farmers' cars at the side of the road to show that they had driven to work in them.

Back at Yalluna I went on to the payroll at 7/6 per week and stayed there until I left to enlist.

Verco Whyte enlisted on 12 May 1918 when he was eighteen years old. A private in the 6th General Reinforcements he embarked on the troopship S.S. *Boonah* on 22 October and reached the port of Durban on 10 November. The ship was immediately quarantined because of an outbreak of Spanish influenza and was still in quarantine when it arrived back in Fremantle with a rapidly diminishing company on 11 December, a month after the Armistice was declared. On 31 January 1919 Verco was discharged from the A.I.F. owing to the cessation of hostilites and soon afterwards he went to work at Albemarle.

Verco Whyte at Albermarle, 1927.

The Albermarle Wages book for week ending January 31 1925 showing that James Hole (top), E.V. Whyte (third from top), Arthur Upfield (9th from bottom) and Syd Whyte (5th from bottom) were working there.

4.

ALBERMARLE

When Arthur Upfield came to Albemarle in 1922, the station covered an area of 732,000 acres (296,240 hectares), extending eastward from the Darling for eighty miles (129 kilometres). It was owned by an Irishman, Captain Alan Ferguson of Limerick, a kinsman of the pioneer squatter James Joseph Phelps, but although Upfield referred critically to absentee owners, it was not run like the station A. B. Paterson lamented where

> The gardens gone; for no pretence
> Must hinder cutting down expense;
> The homestead that we held so dear
> Contains a half-paid overseer
> On Kiley's Run.

The Manager of Albemarle, James L. Hole, a big, able, good-natured man, received a salary of 600 pounds a year, as well as board for himself and his wife and family, and his overseers 200 pounds a year with board; and when one of them left at the end of 1922 to live on a western lands lease he had been granted further east, he was given 2,000 ewes to stock it.

Verco Whyte applied for his position, supported by the recommendation of the boss:

Albemarle, Menindie, N.S.W. Dec. 14th, 1922

The bearer E.V. Whyte has been employed here for the past 4 years. He has had a very fair experience among stock, is a good horseman, and has had a good working knowledge of oil engines, pumps etc. He has been in charge of men and is quite competent to fill an Overseers position. I have no hesitation in recommending him as being one of the best young fellows I have had with me.

Signed Jas. L. Hole

Verco was duly promoted and his name remained on the wages book until 31 August, 1927. The station ran 35,777 sheep, 313 cattle and 160 horses according to the stock return for 1925 and employed thirty-five men and the wife of one of them, as well as paying £2/3/4 every month to a widow. Nothing was skimped. Food was plentiful, the men were well paid and all expenses neatly recorded by a bookkeeper earning 133 shillings a month.

Upfield's initial wage of 48 shillings a week with keep was increased to 135 pounds a year by 1925, the same as that of Tom Randles, Harry Vigar, the tool maker and mechanic, and most of the other hands, and it was increased to 56s.8d. in 1926.

George Cabbage from the aboriginal settlement down the river and the jackeroo, Verco Whyte's stepbrother Sid, both received 40s. a week in 1925. Later two more aborigines were employed, Pluto, who was paid 40s. and Tommy Pluto 25s. He appeared in one of Upfield's books, *The Bachelors of Broken Hill*, disguised as Ted Pluto, "a fine horseman and a fairly reliable stockman… Dressed in gabardine trousers and white silk shirt and with gleaming brown shoes on his slightly pigeon-toed feet." That was the "Sunday best" all stockmen wore when they went on the spree in Menindee or Broken Hill but as aborigines were not allowed to have alcohol then they did not suffer the same hangover afterwards.

The frontage country of Albemarle was first stocked with sheep in 1850 by a Scottish settler Alan McCallum, who had flocks on both sides of the river. His friends, John McKinley of Balurang (later Ki Downs Station) and Edmund Morey of Euston Station, had cattle farther north at Weinteriga west of the river and Tintanollogy on the east. Riding from Tintanollogy hut in search of a stockman who had bolted, Morey saw country similar to parts of Albemarle and described the pleasures of being a pioneer:

"My furthest east brought me to extensive, low-lying flats covered with sweet-smelling clover and from the appearance of the country I inferred that at times water must cover these flats … I afterwards learnt my furthest east must have been within two or three miles from Lake

Terrawania, a large body of water fed by an anabranch, whose intake was many miles up the Darling and named 'Telluwolka' Creek by the natives.

"Evening coming on, I rode south-west until a good claypan at the foot of a pretty clump of pines offered a suitable camp for the night, and there on a bed of sweet-smelling pine needles I passed a restful night.

"Recalling as I do now these long-past incidents, the perfume of the sandal wood or pine camp-fires seems to salute my nostrils, and my pulses stir as I recall the youthful vigour with which I arose from those open-air camps, and the hearty appetite with which I attended my breakfast...

"To me, as doubtless to others under the same conditions, it was a great pleasure to ride over fine, pastoral country never before seen by white men, and more particularly so when the country I was passing over was portion of the run I had secured. Every rising ground was looked at with interest to learn what was beyond and the day was never too long for such interesting rides."

At the beginning of 1852, blacks attacked the northern stations, spearing cattle and killing two stockmen Morey had left in charge. He and other stockholders appealed to the Colonial Government for police protection, and Major Lockyer and a constable were sent to recruit some native troopers and establish a police station on the eastern bank of the Darling at Menindee.

The land in the region was surveyed, divided into runs and advertised for lease by tender in the government gazettes. The lands department, in bellicose mood, named runs after the battlefields of the Crimean War which England was fighting from 1854 to 1856, and even celebrated victorious generals and battles of the past such as Albemarle and Blenheim. The frontage runs so named and another one, each of 32,000 acres, were leased in 1855 to the Irish Quakers James Joseph Phelps and John Leckie Phelps, who also held runs farther down the river, including Pooncarie, Tarcoola, Pan Ban and Lethero. Their Albermarle holding was gradually extended until it consisted of eighteen runs varying in size from 32,000 acres to 65,000 acres, a total of 738,182 acres (298,742 hectares) of leasehold.

The police camp and its horse paddock remained in the south-west corner of the Blenheim run until 1860. Then the police moved across the river to a site near the inn, a low slab building with a thatched roof, and the store which had been established by Captain Cadell when he made the first voyage up the Darling in his paddle steamer *Albury* in 1859. Phelps bought the dilapidated police huts for £100 and used the material for buildings on Albemarle.

On 1 January 1861 a post office was opened in the village but like the police station it was named Perry after the Crown Lands Commissioner. In March 1866, J. J. Phelps, who represented the vast district of Balranald in the legislative council, wrote to the postal department complaining that the continuous use of the name "could perhaps lead to the eventual loss of that beautiful native name, Menindie". The name was changed in June, and many years later in 1918 the spelling was altered to Menindee.

An American riverman, Gus Pierce[3], wrote of it in the 1860's:

"Menindie was then in a primitive state; it consisted of a few huts collected about a barroom and a blacksmith shop ...The hotel was of the roughest. Its bar was nothing more than a couple of unplaned planks supported by four rough-hewn logs, and the ceiling was formed of calico, which had ripped from its fastening in places and sagged in the centre."

The first station huts would have been equally primitive, but in the 1920s the Hole family lived in a fine old pise homestead with a central hall and large, lofty rooms opening through French windows to the surrounding verandahs. Another Irishman from Limerick, Nicholas Sadleir, had managed the station from 1862 until his death in 1908 and supervised a succession of improvements - buildings, fences, yards, dams, wells, sluices, pumps, bridges and rabbit netting. In 1872 the owners of

Albemarle, Teryawynia and Tolarno built a massive earth dam costing £3,000 across the Talyawalka Anabranch just below the intake of the Teryawynia Creek with the intention of forcing water into the latter to fill the lake mentioned by Morey and flow out through wide tree-lined channels to a chain of lakes on Albermarle and the Boolaboolka country of Tolarno.

An outstation was built on Victoria Lake, fifty miles east of the homestead, and in 1867 and '68 a contractor, Wheeler, sank the well which was named after him on a small plain surrounded by low sandhills halfway between the lake and the homestead. After his return to Albemarle in the summer of 1924, Arthur Upfied became the hut keeper at Wheeler's Well, looking after the windmills and cooking for the stockmen who camped in one of the two pine-log huts when they were mustering sheep for shearing and driving them to the wool shed on the frontage.

Upfield lived in the hut which served as kitchen, dining room and living room. At last he had the time and solitude he needed to continue his writing. He ordered reams of foolscap and a fountain pen from Melbourne and sat at his kitchen table scribbling furiously for hours at a time. Once a week he waited impatiently for Verco Whyte to drive out from the homestead in a Ford buck board with rations and a bundle of mail containing copies of *World Wide Magazine* and *The Times Literary Supplement* which he had asked his mother to send from England. In one copy he read a small advertisement inserted by a man in Buckinghamshire named George Frankland, offering to criticise manuscripts and present them to publishers. He answered it and so began an association which continued until Frankland's death fourteen years later.

It was at Wheeler's Well that Upfield wrote and rewrote *The Barrakee Mystery* which introduced his aboriginal detective Napoleon Bonaparte. When it was published in 1929 Verco received a copy inscribed: "To E. V. Whyte trusting that with in these covers many familiar scenes will be discovered".

A visit to Wheeler's Well about 1924.

The Pluto family at Albermarle in the early 1920s.

The novelist's name does not appear on the old wages books after 30 November 1926, but he was still camping on Albemarle and the nearby stations of Teryawynia and Tintanollogy trapping rabbits. They had increased to plague proportions during the good seasons following the heavy rains of 1921, when the lakes had been filled by an overflow of floodwater from the Darling.

Verco Whyte, meanwhile, had married Maud Frey, the bush nurse at Menindee and, like Upfield's wife, a former nursing sister of the Australian Army Nursing Service. After their wedding they lived at Victoria Lake until the end of August 1927, then with their baby daughter Patricia they travelled south to Willow Point Station on the Great Anabranch of the Darling River, where Verco was engaged as manager for four years by the trustees of the estate of L. G. Wheeldon until his son Jock Wheeldon came of age.

By the end of 1927 drought had come again to the river country and the rabbits and kangaroos were dying. Upfield was camped beside a wire suspension bridge between Victoria Lake and Brummy's Lake when he wrote his last letter from Albemarle, casually announcing the acceptance of his first novel by an English publishing company:

Albemarle Stn., Menindee.
12 November 1927

Dear Mr Whyte,

Your letter reached Tintin whilst I was down in Victoria paying my respects to my poor wife. Distance, I verily believe, makes the heart grow fonder, and a separation of a few years is highly to be recommended as an occasional alternative to a weekly thrashing - women are like motor cars. Once you understand them a speed of fifty miles an hour may be reached.

Mr William Dawes is now with me as my assistant. We are camped at the Wire Bridge and are barely making expenses 'kangarooing'. Whilst writing Bill is watching the cattle getting bogged trying to reach a pool of mud at the wire bridge end of the hole.

There is some two feet of water at Surveyors, some eight inches at Galvanised Corner, the same in the big tank at Wild Horse, while the catch tank at Lime Kiln is full, but none in the big tank. I believe the sheep, till recently, fed on the river, are now on their way to Wallace Lake and Wards Dam.

The recent rain has brought up good feed along the outer two hundred yards round the lakes and another rain would do a lot of good. But off the lakes the little feed there is, is quickly drying off and if no rain falls before Xmas conditions here will, I think, be bad. No rain fell at Tintin and the whole place is a dust heap. Terywinia (how the devil do you spell it) is quite as bad. In fact the whole state is done.

William and I are going to W.A. next month. I am selling my car and we are buying a Chev ton truck which I shall drive over, via Eucla.

At last it seems I am getting a market for my writing. Frankland has sold an article on camels to *Tropical Life* for £1/1/0, an article on motor travelling to *Overseas Mag.* for £1/1/0, a fifteen thousand word serial article to *Wide World Mag.* for £2 and greatest of all, he has found a publisher for *The House of Cain*. I do not know what terms he secured for the novel but I am now having dreams of some day being able to earn sufficient with my pen to make me independent of rabbits, foxes and roos, and raise me from the gutter in which I have been so long.

Working on stations and camping under Wire Bridges is quite all right as an experience, but eventually it begins to bore, and the lack of decent food on a well-furnished table begins to make itself felt.

I trust you like your new, home.

Archie Cook is now at Surveyors Lake pumping. He has the Ford Ton with him, but believe they are taking it away for fear he may be tempted to go to Ivanhoe at Xmas. The two Quinns and Wally are here under Mr Harrison. Neil is at the Cocket. We are at Wire Bridge - Dam the Wire Bridge. William Dawes says; that now the rabbits are gone Albemarle is done. I almost believe he is right.

Au revoir. I would be glad to hear from you when you have a writing fit. Please give my regards to Mrs Whyte.

Sincerely yours

Arthur W Upfield.

P.S. Why not keep my letters and when I am dead publish them in a book of memoirs. You could call it *The Life of Arthur the Rabbiter*.

5.

LETTERS FROM THE WEST

Arthur Upfield set off for Western Australia in December 1927 and worked in the bush for another four or five years before he was able to make writing his livelhood. He still found time to write letters to E. V. Whyte, but accustomed as he was to the hierarchy of a station, he did not find it easy to begin calling his former overseer by his Christian name as he requested. The squatter and his manager, overseers and bookkeeper were always given the title "Mister", a form of respect for those in authority which assisted the orderly running of an isolated station with a large workforce of diverse individuals. It was particularly important in the early days of settlement as Captain Francis Cadell indicated in a letter he wrote to one of his riverboat masters, Captain George Johnston in 1856, when pastoral holdings like Albemarle were being established:

"I am glad to hear from various quarters that the Settlers on the Rivers are well pleased with you as a Master but you must be careful when speaking of them to the men always to do so with a handle to their names".

The conventional did not hinder the development of true democracy in the bush where everyone was thought to be worthy of respect and consideration.

A letter from his friend was waiting for Upfield when he reached Perth and he replied immediately:

Arthur Upfield at Albermarle.

Riverside Post Office, Perth.   W.A.
19th Dec 1927,

Dear Mr Whyte,

Your long interesting letter dated 27.11.27 was sent on to me here and I received it yesterday upon arrival.

I am glad to hear that you find in Willow Point an outlet for your organising abilities and I agree with you that to have the opportunity of improving one's own property would indeed be pleasant.

Sweet William and I had a very excellent trip of 2274 miles with no mechanical trouble and only two punctures. After leaving Port Augusta we went south to Cowell, went to Port Esslington (Elliston) and north to Port Kenny and the various bays to Fowler's Bay where we loaded up with five cases petrol at £1 per case (still) and 4 gallons oil at 6/6 per gallon for the seven hundred miles to Norseman W.A. We could have bought petrol at two stations but at £2 per case, and as that was a Warren de la Albermarle there was nothing doing. (Warren was the bookkeeper at Albemarle then).

The wheat crops about Fowler's Bay appeared good. The country across the Nullabor Plain, looked excellent. Plenty of good class saltbush with patches of spargrass. But west of Eucla, between Madura and Belladona Stations, some 205 miles (country vacant), we came through miles and miles of grass as clear of scrub and wood as a wheat paddock.

Enquiries of various people pointed to the fly in the ointment - which was water. There are no creeks and the water does not appear to run over the limestone and ironstone country. There is plenty of water for travellers, water sheds every twenty miles or so. Built by the Government for the telegraph linesmen.

E.V. Whyte around 1926, photographed at Menindee.

At Eucla we found no-one, the postal people having been moved to Cook on the train line. There were, however, three goats living in the Government buildings. The buildings are of stone and appear quite new... They are situated about half a mile from the short jetty. The rail way line exists from the jetty to a large shed, but now it is in places buried by great sandhills.

We stayed at Eucla three days and fished, but caught only gummy sharks and one red shark which could not be landed.

After leaving Norseman we travelled south to Esperance Bay, a place I would like to retire to. The bay and coastline is protected by a group of 105 islands named Research. Some are owned by sheep people.

One has the monkey face kangaroo, a species I would much like to see, another produces pure black rabbits. On yet another mutton birds breed every year and on another thousands of geese find sanctuary.

Oh for money and a good motor boat!

I could write a lot about Esperance Bay.

The wheat harvest in this state is excellent. We saw 8, 9 and 10 bag crops on land which could be bought at £5 per acre. Unenclosed land, miles of it, about Lake Grace for 9/- per acre. Alas, I am getting old and my enthusiasm for work decreases annually,

I have before me Hutchinson's agreement and knowing you will be interested I am sending you Frankland's copy which you can return at leisure. Frank 1 and says that the terms are very good. He tells me I am to get six presentation copies and as he is sending me three I will send you one.

It has to be published in January.

I would so like if you would send me any reviews of the novel you may come across, favourable or unfavourable. Everyone appears to be disappointed that Squeezem Harry only appears in one chapter and Frankland wants me to write another yarn of Monty Sherwood, giving Harry equal prominence.

If only I had the money and the time to settle.

Instead of which I have to go catching rabbits with William.

A letter reached me today from *Life* enclosing a cheque for £3.3.0 for a yarn I sent them over twelve months ago called 'The Man Who Liked Work.' The editor says he regrets the delay but that the story was overlooked and now appears in the December issue so expect that it will come out in January.

It is all very strange. But the cheque is real enough. The only fault is the smallness of the amount.

Before leaving Broken Hill I purchased a Graflex camera for £17.10.0 and made some fifty exposures of the trip. The films and plates are now being developed and I will send on a few interesting prints. As I have taken extensive notes daily I hope eventually to make a few shillings out of it.

Well, well I'm staying at this address, Bill's sister owns the property. We are three miles from Perth G.P.O. but the heat is about 110. Esperence! Oh lovely Esperence - how I love thee!

I trust you and yours are well. Au revoir.

Sincerely yours,

Arthur W. Upfield

Expect *Wide World* articles to start appearing in February. Will let you know when.

Upfield went scrub clearing in the south-west of the state, visiting the isolated lighthouse at Cape Leeuwin, and then trapped rabbits around Merridin east of Perth and at Dongera on the coast, the scene of his novel *The Beach of Atonement*. His first two books were published and he sent copies to Verco Whyte at Willow Point.

Rivervale Post Office,
Perth. W. Aust.
12 March 1928

Dear Mr Whyte

Herewith a copy of *The House of Cain* which I trust will please.

The cover design, though striking, is nothing like the House itself.

The publishers' description of the tale is too flowery, and apt to intensify the reader's final disappointment. However, it is a step on the road.

William and I are starting off for the rabbits tomorrow. We have been in Perth during the last ten days, he staying with his sister who runs the above post office and I at my own home where my wife and son are established.

I am very glad to read that your drought is at least broken and I trust you will experience a few good seasons As I do not like W.A. I shall return to N.S. Wales probably next year, and if near Wentworth will take the pleasure of calling upon you.

Please let me know what you think of *H of C* and send me any reviews you come across. At the end of this month I hope to be in receipt of Frankland's report on my next novel.   Would you growl much if I sent you a typed copy for criticism?

Trusting you and yours are all well. I am

Yours very sincerely

Arthur W. Upfield.

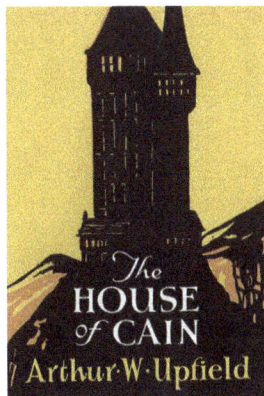

Rivervale P.O. Perth
28th May, 28

Just a short note to enquire if you received the copy of *The House of Cain* sent you from Perth about April 10. Not hearing from you makes me suspect it has gone astray in the post.

The book has been well received in England, much better than I anticipated. Of the dozens of reviews sent me none were bad and that of the *Morning Post,* London only was cynical. It said "The credibility of the House of Cain is as remote as that establishment is from civilisation." *The Times Literary Supplement* "It is a remarkable and original story ably told." *The Hampshire Telegraph* "So well written and so well planned that it is difficult to believe it is a first effort." *The Daily Mirror* "There are thrills in plenty in this gripping yarn."

If the Australian Press give me as good a go I shall be delighted. My adviser in England has just reported on the MS of my next "The Sin of Silence" [renamed *The Barrakee Mystery*] and says he likes it much better than *The House of Cain.* He predicts that with those two novels out my literary future should be assured. I sincerely hope because I prefer writing to rabbiting.

Times are hard and W(illiam) Dawes and I are just scratching, The thousands of little bunnies cause us to hope that we shall do much better after August.

Trusting you and yours are fit I am, as always,
Yours sincerely,
Arthur W. Upfield

The Rabbit Department

Burracoppin W. A. 20th May 1929

I have to thank you for the nice things you have to say about *The Barrakee Mystery*. It seems, to have taken popular fancy in the old country and the twenty-five reviews are better than I ever dreamed of having, I builded better than I knew.

In my last mail Hutchinson's informed me that both books have been accepted for publication in America by Durrance and Co, one of America's best publishing firms. Already it has suggested that I write another Bony story. The third novel called The Princess of Rufus Rocks is being reported upon. It is an ala *House of Cain* with Squeezem Harry as the chief hero. Just now I am writing the last few chapters of the fourth - *The Beach of Atonement*. This work is more in the nature of an experiment. The critics will either damn it and advise its banning or they will acclaim it as the best novel published since the War. There will be no middle course.

I am now in a good billet. I am in charge of a Government Camel Depot of some 400,000 acres, with an excellent four-roomed stone house to live in, When necessary I "put on" a half-caste black to help in breaking in young camels, but that is seldom and the ordinary work of getting fresh camels ready for the boundary riders does not require help. Most of the time I am alone, and at night I make my pen fly. I am glad to hear you are getting in with the Bully.

What did you think of *Coonardoo*?[4] Over here they all howled it down. I read parts. *Barrakee* would have beaten it if it had been put in and the competition been fair which it was not. No regular contributor stood a chance. The *nom-de-plume* business is all a farce. The style in which a MS is written shrieks its author's name.

Under separate cover I am sending you some postcards. Hutchinsons are booming the book. They printed 20,000 of these cards and have sent me a thousand. Would you be good enough to slip one in your personal correspondence. I have yet a long way to go to reach the top of the hill.

During this month over three inches of rain fell here. It passed over east and I trust you got some of it. It must be worrying as well as heartbreaking to watch the poor sheep becoming thinner and thinner.

Congratulations on the heir[5]. My lad is now eight years. His schooling costs me two pounds a week. Thank heaven I haven't ten.

To Xmas last year *Cain* sold to 2280 7/6 copies. As *Barrakee* has been so much better received, plus the fact that both books will see the U.S.A., I am hoping now to become independent of bush work in about a year hence. Life is a funny affair. I quite expect that when that time does come that a relative will obligingly die and leave me ten thousand or I shall win twenty thousand in Tatts. Fortune never smiles only once.

Hoping that you and yours are well, believe me to be always
Sincerely yours
Arthur W. Upfield.

P.S. Barrakee Station was drawn principally from Albemarle. The location to the west of the river above Wilcannia was done to avoid risk of libel. Bony[6] was a half-caste nig I met in Queensland. Blair was my first bush boss on Momba.

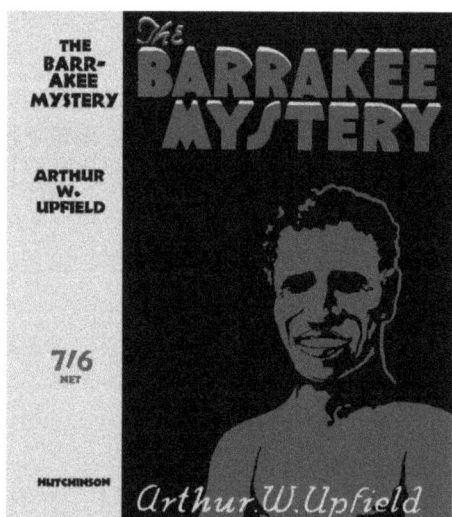

The Rabbit Department, Burracoppin.

25th February 1930

Whilst staying with my family in the hills east of Perth I saw by the paper that you were having some rain over your way at long last. I do hope it will mean the end of the drought, because if you get drought and a 50% cut in wool prices; conditions will become somewhat strained.

I shall be sending you a copy of the next novel to be called *The Beach of Atonement* and trust you will like it. It is a story of murder and seduction in Perth and beachcombing on the north west coast. My literary guide in England thinks a lot of it and says that 1t is a great advance on the former two. I do hope so, and also, hope it will forward my name among the public.

The book should reach Australia at the end of April.

I have written to Heslop, Broken Hill, about this and suggested to him that he buy some copies. Should he do so he will I am sure make a fortune.

Conditions over here are bad and threaten to become worse as the winter approaches. All improvement work on the stations has ceased, and most of the regular hands have been sacked. In Perth the number of unemployed is staggering. They mass at every street corner, and for once it is absurd for the politicians to urge them to go to the country for work. There is now no work even in the country. And I am very thankful that I have a job.

In a shop window I saw this portable Underwood and going within was told that the price was £20 cash or 21 pounds terms - four pounds down and one pound a month. In the end I had four pounds worth. I trust you will be able to read this letter better than my handwriting. Anyway I used it to write an article for the *West Australian* and received two pounds, five shillings, so that the instalments for next two months are assured.

Hoping that you are keeping fit and that Mrs Whyte and the children are well, I am, as always

Yours very sincerely, Arthur W Upfield.

The hastily written letter were sometimes difficult to read and Verco scribbled a comment on the one above, "First typed letter received from him. I hope it will not be the last." At that time Verco's pars about bush life were appearing in the *Bulletin,* or, its popular *Aboriginalities* page, described in verse:

Aboriginalities tell of grim fatalities
Fiction and realities,
Scribes galore,
Things that choke and things that smother,
Fratricide by bullock's brother,
Snakes that swallow one another
By the score.

Arthur, on the other hand, received no encouragement from the Bushman's Bible, which he had read assiduously since he arrived in Australia, and its neglect rankled.

As early as 1903, the *Bulletin* had been described by the *London Times* as "the nurse and the critic, sometimes severe and sometimes friendly, of every young Australian who wants to write about the things he feels and sees. It will print and pay for anything connected with Australia that is put clearly or well said, be it love verse, a snake story or note on the habits of a blackfellow tribe." It was not until Arthur Upfield was an established author that his work was published by "that rag" as he called it. Perhaps he was affronted by its mordant criticism or the editor may have been put off by his first book *The House of Cain,* a thriller in the style of the best-selling novelist, Edgar Wallace. It was, awkwardly written, self-conscious and melodramatic and although set in Australia lacked the "true Australian voice" The *Bulletin* encouraged. In his later books such as *Mr Jelly's Business,* set in Burracoppin, he found a simpler, more straightforward style and his ear for dialogue improved as he wrote about the ordinary men and women he had known in the bush.

E. V .Whyte 's story of one of the men on Albemarle was printed in the *Bulletin* under his pseudonym "Bush-cat" [7]:

Paddy

He was bullock driving on Albemarle when I first met him. That was in 1919 and he was "Old Paddy" then. How old I don't know and I'm doubtful if Paddy did. He was quite illiterate, and having a permanent limp, together with his scrubby grey beard and stooping shoulders, made him appear old. Probably the life he had led had also aged him prematurely, because it had been really hard: working, living and drinking, Paddy had spared himself at none.

His wife was a fitting companion and used to carry her swag along the Darling. Their meeting and marriage is a story in itself. At the time Paddy was cutting firewood for the steamers and had fallen from a tree with the branch he had cut off. Everyone said of course that he stood on the wrong side of the cut, but however he did it he broke his leg and while he lay helpless in his tent where he had crawled, our heroine came along carrying her swag and she remained and nursed him until he could get about again. Then in Paddy's own words he "had to marry the woman or else the neighbours would be talkin'."

They were married by the Sergeant of Police in Menindee, and after the wedding the bride and groom accompanied by the best man left by sulky for their camp on the river. Probably because she was best able to balance there the bride sat in the carrier on the back, but getting up the bank of the Darling after crossing in the punt, the back band of the harness broke and the sulky tipped up spilling them all out. No one was hurt and the chief concern seemed to be for the "supplies", which were also retrieved without spilling or breaking.

There were several gates to go through and refreshments were taken according to custom. When the party arrived at the camp only the bride was missing, so as it was now dark there was nothing for it but to finish the party without her. Next morning it was found that she had fallen out several miles back and rather than walk on had spent the night with some woodcutters camped nearby.

Because of his accident, Paddy had to give up woodcutting and it was then that he started work on Albemarle. He was a good bullock driver and carried on with the aid of an old bay mare and a blue heeler cattle dog. Certainly he was a circus on his own at times, especially when he got bogged and after flailing the leaders with whip and tongue had to hobble back to the polers, giving a forceful reminder of their duties to each pair as he went.

Although a good worker, he could hardly be classed as reliable while the Roseborough Hotel was only a mile away from the homestead and situated in the bullock paddock. If he weren't yoked up by 8.30 when the boss came out from breakfast, someone would be sent to look for him. Their first objective would be the Roseborough, where as likely as not the old bay mare would be hitched up outside and Paddy inside having a few drinks. Sometimes, although he had been at the pub, he would have gone on after the bullocks, and on one particular occasion the overseer, knowing he had taken a bottle with him, went in search of him and found the old mare feeding quietly in a circle and Paddy on his back dead drunk being gently towed around by his foot still caught in the stirrup.

On another occasion when the bullock dray had not turned up at one of the out camps the overseer rode out along the track and found him. He was lying under the dray fast asleep, and while the wheel of the dray was not six inches from his head the ever patient bullocks were gradually twisting it nearer as they shifted their positions to ease the burden of their yokes.

In the end the station bought the Roseborough and surrendered the licence because Paddy was not the only one who could not keep away from it. After pulling down the outbuildings and most of the rooms, there were left three rooms where Paddy and his wife lived, and the only time they left the path of sobriety was when they could bribe someone to bring supplies from Menindee. When this happened they would both go on the spree and Mrs Paddy would become a menace. She would insist on going up to the homestead to see the "Missus" and to complain that "Paddy was trying to kill me." On one very hot day she was seen heading towards the house and a jackaroo was sent to stop her. She was dressed in nothing but a bedspread which was draped around her shoulders and dragged in the bindi-eyes behind. The jackaroo retreated.

Although the T model Fords were beginning to invade the outback then, Paddy did not progress mechanically. All he knew about "them cars" was "where you put the water in the boiler" and "the handle in front you turned to start them up." His introduction to a car had been painful. As the boss tinkered with the engine Paddy came up and placed both his bare forearms on the hot radiator. "Jesus! Holy Jesus!" he said with anguish and due reverence in his voice. He gave such an involuntary jerk to his body that his old slouch hat was dislodged. It was the first time we realised that he was nearly bald, for his old greasy felt was part and parcel of him, together with his patched dungarees with a belt made from bullock hide and his grey striped shirt. As much a part of him also was the cattle bitch at his heels, and my outstanding picture of him is limping from the killing pen in the evening as he made off across the flat to his home. A freshly killed "pluck" gripped by the gullet and dangling against his legs as he walked, and the old bitch following step by step.

Both he and his wife have been dead many years. As kindly a pair as ever lived but having human frailties. May their souls rest.

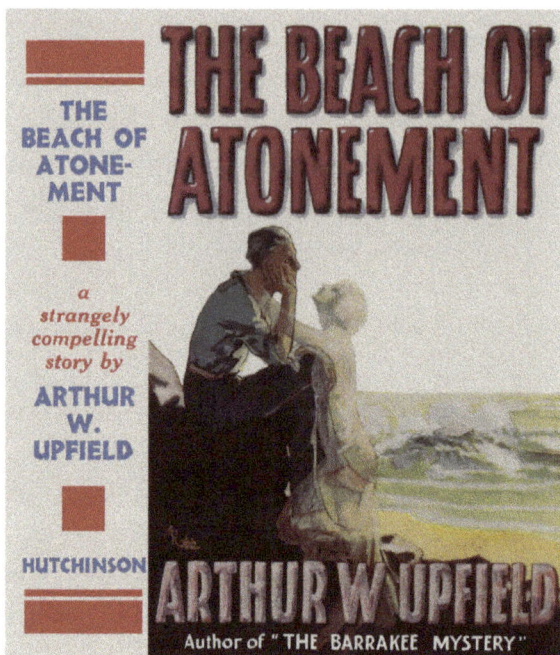

THE
BEACH OF
ATONE-
MENT

a
strangely
compelling
story by

ARTHUR
W.
UPFIELD

HUTCHINSON

THE BEACH OF ATONEMENT

ARTHUR W UPFIELD

Author of "THE BARRAKEE MYSTERY"

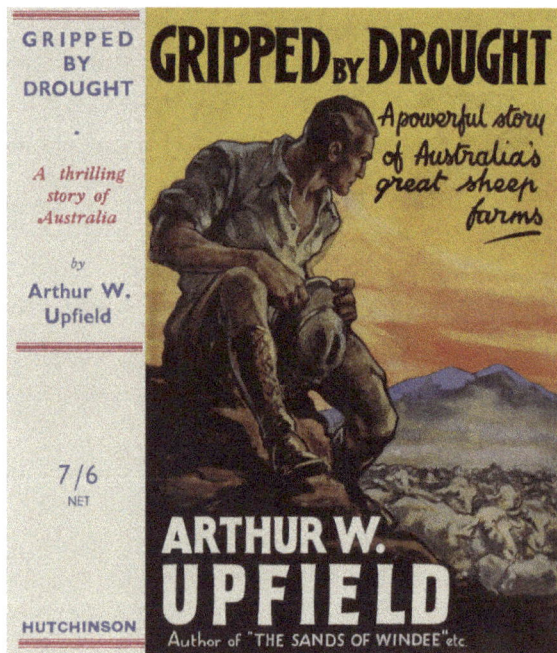

GRIPPED
BY
DROUGHT

·

A thrilling
story of
Australia

by
Arthur W.
Upfield

7/6
NET

HUTCHINSON

GRIPPED BY DROUGHT

A powerful story
of Australia's
great sheep
farms

ARTHUR W. UPFIELD

Author of "THE SANDS OF WINDEE" etc.

6.

DROUGHT

Upfield remained near Burracoppin on the rabbit fence east of Perth throughout the worst years of the depression which followed the collapse of the New York stock market in 1929, thankful to have a secure position. He planned his novel *Drought* and sought expert advice to make it convincing. At Willow Point on the Great Anabranch, E.V. Whyte, his stepbrother Jeff, and Jock Wheeldon, soon to take over the management of his inheritance, spent their evenings by the steady, white light of an Aladdin pressure lamp, trying to solve the difficult problem of making the hero go broke after three years of drought.

> The Rabbit Department,
> Burracoppin, W.A.
> 25th April 1930.

Dear E.V.

I have to-day sent some postcards advertising the *Beach of Atonement*. I rather like the jacket as a general draw to the buying public, even if it appears a little sentimental. The novel itself I shall be sending when they reach me.

This book is unlike the former two. I wrote it not because I particularly liked writing it but because I am forced to the conclusion that to reach popularity one must follow a path other than that of clean adventure. Nevertheless, you will find *The Beach of Atonement* not as bad as many books which have less originality.

Mixing in my mind for some considerable time is the plot of a novel which is to be called *Drought*. The timing of the plot will occupy three years - the end of the third year coinciding with the end [of] a three years drought. I want to portray drought; the agony of animals, the struggle and heart-break of the sheepmen, the inevitable march of poverty and ruin. Against this background I have a set of people who al so suffer in their lives a period of drought. If you will kindly answer the questions on the accompaning (sic) sheet it would be a great help in this work.

Please let me have your candid opinion of *Atonement.* Apart from the sex interest let me know, what you think of the characters, and get Mrs Whyte's opinion of my women characters, which, coming from a woman, will be of value. Tell me, too, if the descriptive matter is clear enough to give the reader lasting impressions. And if or no you think the descriptive matter is too great in proportion to the action.

Several people as well as reviewers like the descriptive matter in *The Barrakee Mystery,* but I have, to avoid overloading in these days of action, action, and only action. My ambitiion is to create an Australian fiction which, whilst pandering to the public demand for thrills will also imprint on the mind of the reader indelible pictures of this country...

I know of a hundred thousand acre block, 150 miles north of Burracoppin and about forty from a rail head which is for sale for about £100. There is no improvements of any sort, and it would require about £2000 to get it going. How about it?

With regards to Mrs Whyte and yourself believe me,
Sincerely yours,
Arthur W. Upfield.

Questions.

1. What month of this year did your drought break?

2. Assuming that it broke at the beginning of 1930 the action of the story would commence early in 1927. What was the average price of wool for those three years?

3.My sheepman owns half a million acres of leasehold. Fully stocked what number of sheep would the holding carry?

Beginning of 1927 .....
Beginning of 1928 .....
Beginning of 1929 .....
End of drought   .....

Please trace the imaginary loss from the start to the end of the drought, the loss to be drastic. Put yourself in the place of an owner of this area fully stocked at the beginning of 1927, and trace your losses throughout, saving a handfull of ewes by hand feeding. I understand that Albemarle came down from 70,000 to 7,000 once.

4. At the beginning of Drought my sheepman is fairly well off and in no-one's debt. It is the drought which ruins him financially, and when depicting his ruin I must trace it throughout. Allied to the loss of sheep during these years could there be other contributary causes over which he had no control? If so please state them.

5. If the dates of my drought do not coincide with your actual drought please suggest another set of years which would be more suitable. If possible let me know the rainfall is over the period - the readings, I mean. The locality of Drought would be a little south of Cuthero.

6. Any other information you may have would be very valuable.

Albermarle in the early 1920s, lots of sheep, not much to eat.

Burracoppin, W.A.

2nd June 1930.

I have to thank you for your letter of May 19th, and also for the reply to my questionaire. This latter could not be better, and from it I shall be able to build up the structure of the new book to be written after the one at present in hand. The condition of drought will, of course, be the background to the plot which must be sufficiently powerful to lessen its drabness. Again I thank you very much.

No longer do I wonder why Australia is bankrupt. Business people in this country have no desire to make money, and very little idea of making it. *Atonement* was published on April 4th, and early in February I ordered 100 copies from a Perth bookseller, the leading bookseller.

He has not been able to supply them yet, and to my repeated enquiries replies that he awaits stocks from the publishers. It is enough to make a man weep. Here am I struggling with camels in the bush when I should be selling thousands of books in a city, and the fools in the city don't know how to get them. I will send yours directly I get them.

Apparently they are already in the eastern states, for I have seen the book review in *The Australasian* dated May 24th. In case you haven't seen it, I must tell you that there is not one damning word in the review. There is nothing but praise. It says, "Incidentally, Mr Upfield may be said to have written the epic of the rabbit trapper", and finishes with, "This bloke's story is a worthy addition to Australian literature." I am somewhat stunned by this last piece as some of the reviews of *Barrakee* said of that book, "It is not an attempt at literature". All of which seems to indicate that a book is a work of literature if the story appeals to the reviewer, and not on account of its construction and prose.

Would not advise to buy the block of land over here at £2000 or even £200. Its carrying capacity would be about 2,500. The dogs are not as bad as in other parts. Water would be easy to find at seventy. No surface tanks would serve. But why worry with the price of wool at £10 a bale. The other day a neighbouring squatter told me that he was not going to loose (sic) money by taking the wool off the sheeps' backs this winter.

Your fireplace idea is excellent. Identical fireplaces are fittings in the main rooms of my dad's house in pommeyland. In that country the art of making fireplaces is indeed an art. It has to be.

Trusting you and yours are keeping fit, Sincerely yours,
Arthur W. Upfield.

N.B. If you take on the task of growing oranges I shall be reminded of Blair in Barrakee who also had to leave the bush to grow fruit in the Adelaide Hills.

> The Rabbit Department,
> Burracoppin, W.A.
> 4th August 1930.

Very many thanks for your letter of July 21st. I am very glad to receive your opinion of *Atonement,* and sorry to hear that it received the knock.

Opinion of this novel is definitely devided (sic). No opinion is luke-warm. It either is praised or it is damned, but, fortunately for me, the people who have praised it are the reviewers chiefly, especially the Australian reviewers. The bloke who reviewed it in the *West Australian,* I think I sent you a copy, wrote to me congratulating me on the performance and urging me to enter it for The Henry Lawson Literary Society's gold medal. From a publicity point of view I have done very well indeed out of it. From the same point of view I did very badly out of the other two. It is all a little extraordinary.

However, I wrote *Atonement* in the effort to get publicity which I have got. *The Australaisan,* how do you spell it? gave me a thump on the back, and inquiries reached me from a Perth and a Sydney paper asking for particulars and a picture.

The whole problem boiled down is this. Write trash which will please the 'literary blokes' and you will get publicity; write good clean adventure and mystery yarns which will satisfy ordinary clean minded people and your way will be long and lonely. So I have written *Sands of Windee* which is another Bony yarn on the same level as *Barrakee,* I am writing The Great Abduction which will be another *House of Cain*, and I am going to write *Drought* which will be on the style of *Atonement* only much hotter in its plot.

The famous Gerald Gould recently wrote a long article on the mystery of best sellers, or what become best sellers. In the mass nothing distinguishes the best seller or other than one thing. Many of them possess no literary merit. Some are badly written. But all are stamped with one thing and that is a portrayal of suffering. Hence Arnold Dudley suffered because he killed Tracy in a quick clean way. In his place I would not have suffered at all, because Tracy would have died with infinite slowness. Nor would I have gone to that beach and moped, and declined the offer made by Edith Mallory. My actions would have been true to life, human: Dudley's actions were those of a man whose mind was centred upon an ideal.

However, I am more than glad you wrote what was in your mind. The benefit of *Atonement* has already been felt. Hutchinsons have sold out every copy of *Cain* and *Barrakee* and are rushing out a cheaper edition. Great is publicity.

I would very much like to win the Henry Lawson Gold Medal if only to prove that there is in Australia an author who can produce novels without the permission of the *Bulletin*, or the approval of that rag. That class of person who has stated that Throssell and Palmer are great authors are the class which has praised *Atonement.* Only *Atonement* is not my class of novel.

Au revoir. My regards to Mrs Whyte. There is one particular I want in ref. to your notes for *Drought,* and I will write in a week or so. Many thanks. Yours ever,

Arthur W. Upfield.

N.B. Mr Hole likes *Atonement* very much. So does my wife and my mother. My Dad says it is horrible and my brother swears when he thinks of it.

Burracoppin, W.A.
About August 20th '30.

Dear E. V.,

I am in camp fifty miles north of Burracoppin within a nice, comfortable hut, and with nothing to worry about other than the continued ability of the government to pay my wages. It has been raining now for ten hours, and at this season the cockies should be yelling for joy. Still, what is the use when wheat will be down to about 1/6 a bushel this year and next.

Just now I am suffering from a slight annoyance because the fool bookseller in Perth failed to supply my order for foolscap in time for the Inspector to bring it up. Anyway, here is the letter I promised you.

A traveller, passing yesterday on his way to Wiluna, left me a recent paper, and by this I see that Scullin has planked the duty on books, which will about cut down my sales by half. One would think that for one thousand per annum it could be possible to find in Australia a man of common sense and ordinary ability. One would think that there would be at least one such man in the mob at Canberra, a man who would have the gumption, say, of you or I. But no.

A few months ago a Melbourne Literary Society wrote me saying that it was hoped to hold an Australian Book (Show) in London and would I contribute copies of my books. The Federal Government had granted £50 for the cost of such books to be transported to Australia House, where the show would be staged. The idea was to push before the people of England, as well as Australia, the products of Australian literary blokes. In other words to foster Australian literature. And now the party which voted £50 of the peoples money have put a duty on novels which will strangle almost every Australian novelist. The Gov. voted money for an object, and then jumped on it. It beats me.

I expect shortly to have the expert's opinion on *Sands of Windee*, another Bony-cum-station yarn. I am writing just now, when the fool sends my foolscap, a thriller on the lines of *House of Cain*, to be called *The Great Abduction*. Then my attention goes to *Drought*, a copy I hope eventually to send you if just to bore you. In the meantime will you, of your kindness, answer me these relative questions.

In your delination (sic) of a squatter in financial difficulty you say that his expenses during the three years would amount to £118,000 p.a. Can you give me a rough idea how that money would be expended? How much for shearing and carting, and how much living expenses, various taxes and amounts. (just roughly)

Now, my 'ero is an expert sheepman, and, therefore, the author should be an expert sheepman, too. Or at least it is supposed he is. He has built up a fine flock, suitable to the district. Assuming that you inherited a fine pastoral property and had several years to improve the wool as well as the carcass quality what sheep would you mate with what sheep. Of course I require only a bare outline. I have not lost sight of the fact that I shall be writing a drama and not a work on how to run a station.

So far the whole point or reason, according to your paper, why the 'ero fails is that he did not recognise, when a rain came, that the drought was not ended, failing to dispose of his surplus stock when the market temporarily stiffened. To me that is an important point, as the reason why he failed just there can be attributed to the thrice cursed villian (sic). Roughly, the plot is this.

On trip to England the hero married, and returned to his station with the bride, at the start of the drought. The manager of a neighbouring station sets himself to ensnare the bride, and with false advice, plus false vitally important information, succeeds in ruining the bloke to get at the tart. The central idea is to draw a picture of drought as it is imposed on the mind of an alien woman;   the kind of woman who imagined, when she got here, that she would be waited on hand and foot by niggers, and bowed and scraped to by the rest of humanity.

The answers to these questions are not of immediate importance, so do not put off anything for the purpose of answering them at once. However, write a line or two when you feel inclined. I often feel inclined, but cannot spare the time.   I cannot get enough time to write even one novel and a couple of articles in a year. And that certainly is slow going,

Conditions are becoming hellish, ain't they. No-one has any money, and I had a deuce of a job getting rid of the 100 copies of *Atonement* I got especially for people who have been asking me about it months ago.

By the way, if I did not send you the review of this book published by the *West Australian*, I sent two to Mr Hole, asking him to forward you one. The reviewer said that the yarn should have ended when Dudley made atonement, and that the last chapter should never have been written. He was quite right. That last chapter spoilt the whole. I'll profit by that review.

Au revoir. Please remember me to Mrs Whyte. I trust she and your children are all well. The eldest must be five, is she not. Darn it, how quickly we grow old.

Best of wishes,
Always sincerely your,
Arthur W Upfield.

The book appeared at the end of 1932 entitled *Gripped By Drought* because, as the author explained, "the one all-sufficient word Drought" had already been used for a novel in circulation. He dedicated his book: "To my friend E.V. Whyte to whom I am indebted for the pastoral statistics and other data which have made this story possible."

By the time it was published, Arthur Upfield had become well-known for an earlier book, *The Sands of Windee,* not only because it won the Crime Book Society's award but also on account of the macabre events associated with the writing of it.

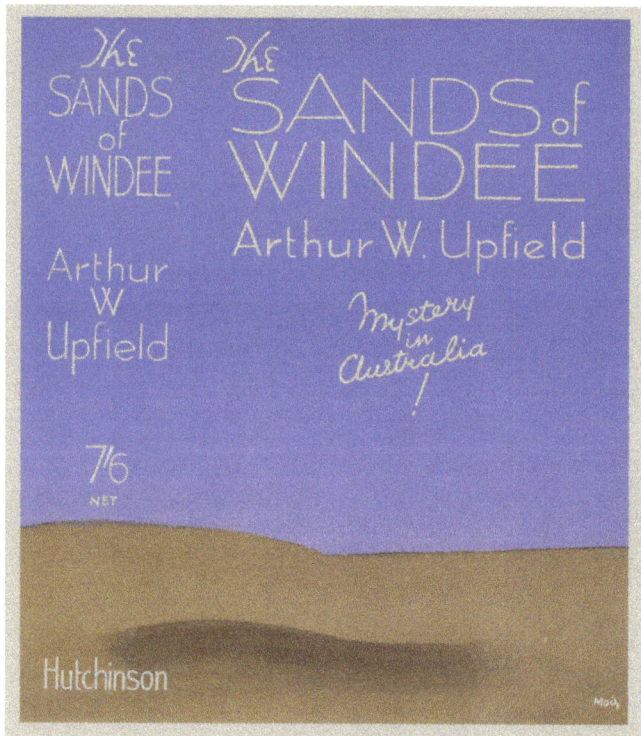

The Sands of Windee
The SANDS of WINDEE
Arthur W. Upfield
Mystery in Australia!
7/6 NET
Hutchinson

7.

THE MURCHISON MYSTERY

At the Government Camel Station fifty miles north of Burracoppin, Upfield wrote a second murder mystery solved by his invincible detective Napoleon Bonaparte. While he was developing the plot he discussed it with the men who called there and inadvertently became involved in a true story of cold-blooded murder. He explained the circumstances in a series of letters written in 1931:

Burracoppin, W.A.

30th March, 1931.

Dear E.V.,

For the last time I am going to annoy you with *Drought* which is nearing completion. Bar subsequent alterations and a little rewriting of parts it ought to do - in fact it should prove to be my masterpiece. Will you please answer the questions sat out in the accompanying sheet, and let me have them as soon as possible.

The Sands of Windee will be the third and therefore the final option novel of my contract with Hutchinson in 1927. I am informed by cable that it will suit but they want to impose on me a new contract binding me to submit two further novels as option novels. What do you know about that? So I have said, 'Yes' provided they agree to publish two novels per annum instead of one as in the past, and as two option novels are practically ready one should get in a heavy burst sooner or later.

My agent says that *A Royal Abduction* - to follow *Windee* - is much superior to *Barrakee* and *Windee,* even to *Cain* which type of yarn it is. *Drought* ought to grip because my "genius" in mixing your facts and figures with love, humour and adventure, plus human charactcrisation, should make it so...

It appears that *Windee* is going to receive enormous publicity. I will tell you a story confidentially at present.

Before writing *Windee* I wanted to go one better than the past and current detective writers whose investigators always start their investigation with a corpse. It is assumed generally that a corpse is an extremely difficult thing to wholly destroy, leaving no trace of it ever having existed. I desired to know an absurdly simple yet utterly effective method of destroying a corpse so that my detective would just have to prove that a man had been murdered and then prove who murdered him.

At that time - 1929 - I was at the Government Camel Station with a gent who had often been in gaol and I put this problem to him with little hope of it being solved. To my amazement he described a method of destroying a body so simply that I am aghast, now that *Windee* is to be published, that everyone will use it upon murdering their enemies.

For remember that in British Law murder has to be proved by the production of the body or identifiable parts of it.

As I have written the procedure of destruction was so simple. Every possible chance of failure was accounted for. It was so simple and so thorough that Bony could not be provided with the ghost of one clue on which to base his investigations. I had to find a clue. And I couldn't. I asked this man and a dozen others to think out how my murderer could make a mistake. They couldn't tell me and only after many months an inspiration provided me with that clue. So the fiction murder was committed, Bony arrived on the scene two months afterwards, proved that the man was dead, had been murdered, and who murdered him.

Now for the sequel.

Among those I asked to provide me with a clue after the assumed murder had taken place was a station hand on the adjoining station named Rolls (Rowles).

In May of last year a man named Garron (Carron) disappeared and Rolls cashed his cheque for £27 at Paynsville (Paynesville). The last seen of Garron was in Rolls company, the latter driving his own car stated to be purchased of Ryan.

Upfield's own photograph of Snowy Rowles with Ryan's utility was used as police evidence in the Murchison Murders case.

This photograph of Ryan's utility shows the rifle and dog owned by Snowy Rowles (Tom Thompson collection).

Ryan and his mate and Rolls stayed one night at the Camel Station arriving the December previous, vis 1929. Rolls then left his station work. As far as can be ascertained I am the last person to have seen Ryan and his mate alive.

The whole Murchison district has been scoured by police hunting up Garron, the first to be reported missing. Now they have just found human bones, teeth and a ring in a fire site twenty miles north of the camel station. Close to the fire site are two heaps of ashes and it is assumed that Rolls murdered Ryan and his mate for Ryan's car, burnt their bodies and sifted the ashes for remains - there faithfully following out my book plot. When he murdered Garron the following May for £27 he took his body and burned it in the same fire site where he destroyed the others, and fatally - for himself - put off returning to the site to sift the ashes for Barron's remains.

I trust I have made myself clear.

All over the Murchison district is the story of my hunt and success for a method of completely destroying a human body. My inspector tells me that the police know of it and says that as I am probably the last person to see Ryan and his mate alive I am almost sure to be drawn into the case. My inspector says I am a damned danger to the human race.

But how on earth was I to know Rolls would act like that? He is a young, well set up, good looking fellow, very popular with everyone. It transpires that his real name is Smith and that he broke gaol where he was for breaking and entering. They are holding him in Fremantle on that charge now.

If Rolls has murdered three men, if it cannot be proved that he killed Ryan and Co because no traces of them are left but it can be proved by human bones, teeth and a ring that he killed Garron, and that the murders were actuated by a novelist's plot, I am not going to get fame but notoriety. In either case *Windee* must sell like hot cakes if it is published to be on sale in Australia at the time of the trial.

Save for the arrest of Rolls on the charge of breaking gaol nothing has so far appeared in the press. Nothing will until the Ds have completed the case. The affair threatens to become the most sensational murder case in the history of Australian crime and I am wondering if to hide my head with shame or shake hands with myself that Fate, plus Rolls, may acquaint lots of people with Arthur W. Upfield.

Anyway I am still smiling - and incidentally thinking out another effective method of destroying a body so that Bony may be able again to make his bow.

Mums the word for the time being.

How are you getting on at Willow Point? I hope you have received a new engagement. It has been a dry summer here but not so frightfully hot as last year. Australia is beginning to bump the rocks, but if we hang all the politicians and appoint a small commission the country will pull through.

Au revoir, write soon the answers to my questions.

If it appears that I am to be put in the witness box I'll let you know. I shall be frightfully nervous and stutter like hell.

Please convey my regards to Mrs Whyte. Hoping all of you are well and cheerful.

Sincerely yours
Arthur W. Upfield

20th May 1931

Dear E.V.

Very many thanks for your prompt dealing with the questions submitted to you, and your long letter which reached me at the same time. I regret to hear you are leaving the pastoral industry and taking up fruit growing, but I hope you will find the change of benefit.

Hutchinsons wanted to buy all rights in *The Sands of Windee*. I declined, insisting on the original basis of royalties. I did so because I think these murders over here will push *Windee*. Anyway, the publishers have climbed down, but I have had to agree to give them the option over my next three novels. They agreed to publish two annually.

We should get *Windee* in Australia about August. As *A Royal Abduction* is considered good it should come out next February, with *Drought* following six months later. This gives me plenty of time to make *Drought* good. Having read the story in two evenings I have been able to see it in its whole, and although I think it good I think it could be made better. As a matter of fact I am never satisfied that what I write could not be improved. I'll let Frankland and have *Drought* for criticism and probably re-write it.

The murder case has gone flat. Nothing is stated about it, but the police are still on the job. We have an idea that the list of murders is not yet complete.

It seems almost certain that this case is going to give me wide publicity. With the help of another man I evolved the Perfect Murder. Rowles when he killed Ryan and Lloyd doubtless followed the method and made of it a perfect murder because they have found no remains of these men. When he murdered Carron, in the following May, he had become careless, and they have enough remains to prove that Carron was burned.

A literary friend of mine in Perth is very friendly with one of the editors of *Smith's Weekly*. My friend says that the inside story of those murders will be worth £100 to Smiths, he proposes I write it and offer it with an article he will write about me and my books. He thinks *Smiths* will boom me on the foundation of having 'discovered' an unknown established author of merit. Still, I would rather the opportunity for publicity came in any other form than through this murder business.

My job still goes on although wages have dropped almost £1 a week. My wife, however, is having extraordinary luck. Her present nursing case has now lasted nine months and looks as though it will last indefinitely. In the Nurses' Club, Perth, the nurses on the list number about fifty and many have had no work for months.

I have lost all patience with the present Federal Labour Government. It is evident that the British financiers have made up their minds not to help us till Scullin & Co have been displaced by their friends the Tories. And unhappily we are not in the position to argue the point and indulge our fancy for politics. Theodore should be behind iron bars. He has done more harm to the working man than did Bruce and all his crowd.

Well, au revoir.

I'll send you a copy of *Windee* in due course.

Remember me please to Mrs Whyte. Hoping you are all well.

Sincerely yours,

Arthur W. Upfield.

Burracoppin, W.A.,
8th June 1931.

Dear E.V.

If I have not thanked you for your last letter dated April 21st I must do so now, yet I have a faint memory of having done so several weeks ago.

The annual two weeks holiday due to me last October, and not taken because my wife has an exceptionally good case, lasting now almost ten months, I am taking them now in a government cottage one mile from Burracoppin.

Commanding perfect peace I have been able to rewrite a lot of Drought, and now send it to my agent really satisfied that, save for possible minor alterations, it will meet with his approval. I shall arrange to forward the carbon copy so that you may read and correct any stupid mistakes which you, as a sheep man, may see, so that the corrections may be made on the original before it is sent to the publisher about this time next year. Personally I like the story.

As per my post card sent a few days ago, *Windee* is to be published on June 19th. Hutchinsons have demanded particulars of my career and photographs, so it would seem that at long last they have decided to try and sell my books. They wanted to buy *Windee* outright as they did *Atonement* and bind me to submitting them my next three books. In reply I refused to sell outright, and agreed to the option novels if they would agree to this and that and the rest. Not a little to my surprise they agreed to everything.

The Murchison Mystery still remains one. I think the difficulty lies in the identification of the remains supposed to be those of Carron. Of the other two nothing has been found, and I think nothing ever will be found. They were killed and their bodies destroyed as per *Windee*.

When Carron's turn came the killer had grown careless, or was unable to obtain the sieve which he easily could have got during the preceding December. I have my story all ready for release directly the trial is over and the sentence given.

One of the conditions got from the publishers was the bringing out of two novels per annum, instead of the one. *A Royal Abduction* should therefore appear next December or January. Of this Frankland says - "In my opinion *Royal Abduction* is certain to be taken, and will raise your stock everywhere." So that should *Drought* prove as good an effort as I think it is I ought to be on my feet shortly after it appears if not before. The consolable feature of this long-delayed recognition of my stupendous cleverness is that when I do strike gold with one book all the others published will also produce gold. And gold is a very necessary commodity just now.

I trust you and yours are keeping fit. I regret that you are leaving wool for fruit, but as you say it may well be a change for the best.

You will chafe at the confinement after the wide spaces of a run. For me to work in a city would be like being in prison. Au revoir.

Let me have your address.

Very sincerely yours, Arthur W. Upfield.

Wages dropped 20/- per week

Work less by 20

> The Rabbit Department
> Burracoppin,
> West Australia.
> 7th July 1931.

Dear E .V.

Just a short note this time thanking you for your kind wishes contained in your recent letter dated June 8th. I was as much surprised at *Windee* getting the blue ribbon of the Crime Book Society as you must have been, because I never have thought much of it from a literary point of view. In future I intend taking out patents on my murder plots, and if any person puts them into actual practice I shall sue them for damages.

I am honestly delighted to hear you are having a record season. It should help N.S.W. if only you can get rid of Lang and Co.

Now I am anxiously waiting for my agent's report on *Drought*. I lay great hopes on that yarn, and I hope it will prove to be far and away my best. I will let you know what he has to say in due course.

Here everyone is broke, and the season appears to be only middling so far. Another poor harvest and 90 of the cockies will walk off their farms.

I hope you and yours are well. Kindly give my regards to Mrs Whyte. You have the advantage over me in having a decent home and a woman to look after you. Au revoir,

Very sincerely yours, Arthur W. Upfield.

In March 1932 John Thomas Smith, alias Snowy Rowles, was tried for the murder of Louis Carron, whose real name was Leslie Brown. Clues found near the heaps of ashes, a gold ring and human teeth with fillings, were proved to be those of the victim by a jeweller and a dentist in New Zealand. During the course of the long trial, Arthur Upfield was called to the witness box to testify about the discussions at the Government Camel Camp in 1929.

John Smith was found guilty and hanged in Fremantle Gaol on the morning of 13 June, 1932.

Australian Crime Series

The **Murchison Murders**

by ARTHUR UPFIELD
(Author of "The Sands of Windee")

6d

EDITED BY
BERNARD CRONIN

In the annals
of crime
there is no
stranger
story than
this.

Published by
THE MIDGET
MASTERPIECE
PUBLISHING CO.
Sydney, Melbourne
London

Upfield duly published his own position on the Snowy Rowles case in a small format stapled edition in 1932.

8.

RETURN TO THE EAST

No longer obliged to struggle with camels in the bush, Upfield went to Melbourne in September, 1933 to begin a six-months contract with the *Herald* and wrote from the office in the new year:

> c/o Herald Feature Service, Herald Building,
> Flinders Street, Melbourne C1
> 4 Jan. 1934.

Dear E.V.

I was most pleased to hear from you and receive your timely well wishes. I have no excuse to offer for not writing before if it is not an excuse to plead rush of work and good intentions only. Believe me, I sincerely hope that this year will prove prosperous to you and will see you well round the corner.

The above address will occasion you some surprise. I am now on the literary staff of the *Herald* having accepted the offer of a six months trial contract writing serials and special articles. Quite a change from cooking at Wheeler's Well, but I sometimes think I would like to be back at Wheeler's Well. Arriving here just before the Melbourne Cup, I was asked to write a racing serial.[8] Bit of a snag that. But I did it although I was not entirely satisfied. Am engaged in re-writing a serial called *Breakaway House* [9] but believe a series of articles concerning my arrival in Australia, breaking-in and subsequent highly-coloured adventures will first appear.

My contract will expire in mid-March, and until I know what will happen I cannot bring my wife and boy over from Perth. The *Herald* chiefs are very peculiar. No one feels safe. They are affable one day and ignore one the next. My single hope lies in establishing myself and making increased chances of being employed by another paper. I do think I am making my way with special articles. I have arranged one a week and most of them have been good enough to be featured in the leader page. One enclosed.

The fool geographic mag. people sent my article back for alteration so there will be a delay in that quarter.

Was pleased to hear that you are still boxing on and that your block is developing. I have no doubt that when the Soviet and Japan go to war things will look up in this country. It is good that wool has risen, and if and when other commodities rise we will probably regard the depression as a bad dream.

If coming to Melbourne be sure to let me know. Just at the moment I am camped in a furnished shack on the top of Mount Dandenong - 2000 ft up.

I suppose Syd is still at Albemarle. Mr Hole wrote some time ago saying that the country was very dry. He's a wonderful man, pulling that place through the depression. Do you remember the evening I told J de C that what was wanted was more taxation for absentee squatters? Didn't he bite.

Well, au revoir. If I last out here I will most likely take a run up through Wentworth and out to Victoria Lake. By that time I will deserve a holiday.

Please remember me to Mrs Whyte. Of the family I saw only the eldest as a baby. Crumbs! How the years fly!

Sincerely yours
Arthur

Mount Dandenong Victoria.
12th February, 1934.

Dear E.V.

I waited for results before replying to your last letter I was very pleased to have.

I spent a free evening writing the article from the details you supplied but it was no go. I think one is up against so many influences in a newspaper - and, too, up against jealousy.

Arthur Upfield (left) helping out with lamb marking at Brummies near Victoria Lake.

The mail truck arriving at Albermarle around 1924.

We will never do any good in this country until we shoot all the politicians. One and all are bloody thieves and worse, and by the way world affairs are progressing many nations appear to have wakened to this fact.

I wrote a series of autobiographical articles which became very popular. They were syndicated in four other papers, and with the extra proceeds I have been able to send for my wife and son. They are now crossing the Bight and being very sick. I am writing this from the above in a small shack , but I have rented a furnished house for them *pro tem*. I go to the city twice a week - an hours run in a service car.

Tommy Randalls is in town. I lunched with him once and he came out to spend a Sunday here. Getting very grey. It was delightful to hear about the old district and the fates of many of the old identities... Tommy is returning next Tuesday.

I have been very busy these last few weeks. Just completed a second series of autobiographical articles and am near completion of another serial called *Breakaway House*.

Since being on the job I have got into the *Herald* 202,000 words which average out at 10,000 a week. Now I am near the end of my six months contract and early next month I shall get the sack or a rise in wages. Note I do not say salary - or returns.

You should get the *Herald* instead of the morning paper. Much more entertaining. I have made it so.

Remember if you come to town to let me know.

Au revoir, Remember me to Mrs Whyte. I hope the family are all well. What the devil I am going to do with my 14-year old son I don't know.

Yours sincerely
Arthur W. Upfield.

Mount Dandenong, Victoria.
29th November, 1934.

Dear E.V.

I have been wanting to write to you for some time, but various jobs had to be done that put me back. You have been in my thoughts on account of the hoppers which appear to be bad up your way, and I sincerely trust you have managed to combat them. It seems remarkable that the stupid Government Department could not have wiped them out before they took to wing, and it is not as though it was the first year they became a plague.

The article I wrote about Victoria lake flopped always, so I am returning your photos as promised. The article I wrote for the *American Geographic* was acceptable, but the pictures I sent, including some very fine ones procured from the Tourist Bureau, Sydney, were turned down, and I flopped on that too.

I severed my connexion (sic) with the *Herald* because they wanted serials written to order and in five minutes and I found I simply could not do it. I was wanting in an Oxford accent which Sir Keith Murdoch demands among or of his hirelings, so that we did not get on very well from the start. I thought it worth more money to cultivate an accent.

Broke out, therefore, on my own, and whilst I have not done so well I have at least retained my self respect. I have done quite a lot of work for the new magazine, *Walkabout*, a copy of the first issue being sent you under separate cover.[10]

And then about a month ago I was approached by a really wealthy squatter to write his biography.[11] He is 84 years old, and looks and acts like a man of 60. Came out here in 1863 on a clipper as an apprentice - cleared out on her second voyage to Australia - went with two other young fellows to the New Hebrides where they fought the savages and had a high old time. Then he returned to Melbourne and got a job for a little while in the Lands Department. Not long satisfied with that, he engaged to survey Albemarle for the purpose of running pumped water outback from the river, and after that was proved to be impossible he went to work on Albemarle as a bookkeeper under Sadlier (sic). What do you know about that for a coincidence?

From Albemarle he went up on the Cooper and formed a station called Monkira for other people, From there he went to the Gulf of Carpentaria and took up land 1878 which he eventually sold for £69,000. For several years he bought and sold stations, and still owns Hughendon Station, outside Charleville. Has now a fine house at South Yarra , and runs a Rolls Royce with a capable chauffeur. I told him his job would be a six months one, and that I would want £300 to do it - payable monthly in advance. Agreed like a bird, and I have been kicking myself ever since for not asking for £1000.

How are you all getting along?   Hope Mrs Whyte and yourself are well.   Your family will be growing up.   My boy is 14, taller than I and wears number eight boots.   Ye Gods!   How the years roll by. Excuse bad typing but I cannot see very well as there is a roaring thunder storm going on. Hooroo - and better times.

Sincerely yours, Arthur W. Upfield

E.V., at his orange grove Riverview on the Darling near Wentworth, longed to return to the pastoral country.   James Hole had written in February:

Albemarle
Menindie,
12th Feb. 1934

My Dear Verco,

Just a line. You will doubtless be surprised to hear that we are leaving Albemarle. My wife has been very ill and the Dr has strongly advised me to get her away from this country altogether. I had to get the Dr out to my wife some time ago, and since then she has been far from well all the time. So it is a case of clearing out, after being here 29 years. I hate the thought of leaving but it has to be, and I will have to make the best of it. We are not leaving till 30th June, and meantime I am trying

Following the 1924 floods, birdlife was abundant around Victoria Lake.

The days catch at Victoria Lake in 1924.

to get a small property in a more favoured district, but it is hard to get what you want. However I may be lucky and drop on to something suitable.

I was in Sydney about a fortnight ago, and did my very best to get you the position as manager here, but they had already picked a man (the cows) though there is nothing absolutely definite about it. I am keeping in touch with matters and will shove your claim along all I can if the opportunity offers, though I am afraid it is a "gone coon".

There is nobody I would have sooner seen here than you and Mrs Whyte, and Mackellar also did what he could for you.

Great feed here now, and we could do with three times the number of sheep.

Excuse the short note but I have a lot of correspondence to attend to.

With kind regards to you all from all here

Yours sincerely,

Jas.L. Hole

As he feared Verco did not get the position, and he was disappointed also about the trip he and Upfield planned to make in two years time, because the latter strained his knee so badly that he was crippled for months. He wrote four letters in 1936:

Mount Dandenong
Vic. 10 May 1936.

Dear E.V.

Well here we are into May, and I fear I have no good news for you if no really bad news...

I am hoping that we will get away early in July and I will be no less disappointed than you if the trip goes up in the air, not only for the sake of the trip but because of the money and time lost.

I have a second or alternative scheme if the round Australia trip has to be put off till next winter. *Walkabout* much desires me to write up and picture the lost expeditions of Burke and Wills and Leichhardt. We could do that in September and October - from five to eight weeks according to the time you could l eave your pl ace at that time of year. As an alternative, how would this suit you?

I was not successful with the Bully humour yarn, but they took a dramatic job I did not expect them to. I had to write A and R (Angus and Robertson) about *Wings above the Diamantina* & they have just replied that they regret delay and now will examine it and will, if they accept the job, have it published simultaneously both in New York & London. I shall be darned grieved if they turn it down especially as the Ed of the *Australian Journal* says it is the most popular yarn among his readers since he has been ed. for ten years or so.

Yes, it is a hell of a gamble, this writing life, but it is very fascinating and there are plans to win. One can only die trying. It seems to have one crooked path which nearly all writers have to top. At the beginning, the hopes and dreams, then the disappointments, then the slow upward stagger and finally - if one doesn't get killed by a war or a motor, average success. So far in Australia, only Idriess has made money. Later I shall, too, I feel it in my blood. Then, every year, other countries are slowly opening up to Australia and its interests.

So au revoir! All your letters I have put aside, and your suggestions will be adopted when the time comes to buy the utility. Remember me to Mrs Whyte. Yours still in hope

Arthur W Upfield

Mount Dandenong, Victoria. 2 July, 1936

Dear E.V.

I have not written because I have been too darned depressed, and feel that I am responsible for hoisting you up only to bring you down with a thud. While I am feeling stronger in myself the knee is wretchedly stubborn despite the treatment called for by the specialist and rigorously applied by my wife. I can manage to walk about a quarter mile, and while I am hopeful that I will get right some day, I am impatient to be right now and not when I am dead.

A super-Pontiac stopped here the other day and in came the editor of *Walkabout* recently returned from his flying tour round the world. He was looking for me to supply him with articles and pictures, and he is still keen for me to do the "Xplorers' Footsteps" articles. When I think of the chance to make money out of him I go cold at not being able to take it.

Still, I am not going to cut my throat - yet.

The gift of oranges will be very greatly appreciated, I can assure you. The fruit trade wants a terrific jolt. Two weeks back my wife got oranges from the local store. They were tough-skinned and juiceless and tasteless. It is the same with apples. If we can't buy apples by the case those in the shops are like sawdust. Many thanks for that case. I will get the carrier to look out for it.

The murder yarn in the Bully was bought and paid for by the last February. They are corkers all right. At other times I have got a cheque in less than a week of submitting and the stuff has been published in 2 weeks. The same yarn caught the eye of Rob Burns in a Sydney barber's shop. Do you remember him?... He was the bloke who went with Syd and me to Adelaide that time Syd took home about half a ton of nardoo stones.

I don't know if you are following my *Wings Above the Diamantina* in the *Australian Journal.* That job has pushed the sales up 1,000 a month and the next job, "Strange Fellows", will begin next January, with a £20 rise. Angus and Robertson are publishing *Wings* as near as possible to September 1st and they have guaranteed to find an English publisher.

They also sought for the right to exploit the cinema rights as they think they can get £500 for *Wings*, they taking 10. I told 'em to "Have a go". Idriess, I understand, is dying of cancer; poor Dixie! If A & R lose him, they will have only Hatfield as a best seller so they may try to push me.[11]

I want you to believe that you cannot possibly be more disappointed than I at not being able to do the round Australia trip this winter. We will do it next winter if alive. This summer we could do Sturt's travels, and have a look at Lake Frome. It will be hellish hot but I think a good roasting would put me on my feet. The point to remember is that I have the money to buy the transport and the sure opportunity to make money with it. The only matter that worries me regarding the future is Hitler. If he starts the world will go bung for good.

Please remember me to Mrs Whyte. Hope all are well

Sincerely yours

Arthur

Mount Dandenong, 8th August, 1936.

Dear E.V.

You will think I am a strange kind of a bird not writing to say how much we appreciated the case oranges. They were excellent, and it was indeed kind of you to send them.

For five weeks now I have been quite helpless with my right leg in plaster of Paris, and only now am allowed to sit up - with the leg still in plaster - so that I can type a note or two in an effort to catch up with the correspondence. Please excuse this abnormally bad writing.

I went to a surgeon-specialist in Collins Street about the knee and he said that while I moved the leg it would never get better. If it is no better when the plaster is removed in another three weeks I will have to have an operation. It seems to beat them all. I wanted him to operate right away, and he said that then he or any other surgeon wouldn't touch it. It is allright, and sometimes I feel like crying with disappointment. All that is left me is the hope that it will be all right for next winter. I told him that sooner than go on being crippled I would have the leg cut off and a cork one fitted. Stiffen the crows! It is now getting on for six months.

The Sands of Windee finished up over the air a week or so back, and Scribe received about 200 letters from listeners about it. It augurs well for the sale of the new job, now appearing in the *Journal*. I have read the letters and my head is now number 12 size. I would be much better pleased if there was less fame and more hard cash. You will have to excuse a short letter this time. It is so damned awkward to write or even use a machine. Hope you are all well.

Yours ever

Arthur W.

Mount Dandenong, Victoria, Monday.

Dear E.V.

Under separate cover I am sending you a copy of the latest job, *Wings Above the Diamantina*. I am pleasureably surprised by the standard of this Australian publication. The cover I like, and the type is well set up and well spaced. The price is much more reasonable than the 7/6 charged for an English book of no superior quality. Let me know what you think about the production. The story is quite plain, it could be written better and there are several printers' errors, which would not have been there had the publishers let me have a set of proofs.

I was pleased to get your letter and to hear you are all well. My knee is still bad, but strangely enough I am much better in myself. In fact I have not been better for years and I have put on at least a stone in weight. The quack wants me to see the specialists again, but I have refused to be "mucked about with" for at least another three weeks as I am busy revising and typing another Bony yarn for the *Australian Journal*. They have put up the price to £100 because *Wings* increased their circulation by 10,000 per month.

With this work off my hands I am determined to get down to serious business with this knee. I am tired of it, and the fool quacks have had a fair spin. Darn it, if I cannot get it straight I shall not be able to drive a car or walk about save on crutches. I am astonished that grown men with hair on their chests and in the possession of medical degrees can't cure a simple complaint like a knee. My wife, as I think I told you, was a nurse, and, she thinks the sun shines extra bright on all quacks. It is very strange how they are able to influence women to believe in their cleverness. My knee is out of joint. I have put it out of joint and formerly was able to work it back. All I want at this stage is a whiff of ether when the leg could be jerked straight with a hard tug, but the fool quacks measure it with a tape measure, prod it about and look wise. I reckon if I could be put in the middle of a big paddock and a mad bull loosed on me so I would have to run like hell that the leg would go straight automatically. Unfortunately there are no bulls, mad or sane, around here.

When I get the utility I think it will be an International with 19-inch wheels to give a good clearance. I will get it new to save the other bloke's troubles. If the leg remains crook till late this year, I will wait till next year before buying in order to get the 1937 model.

I will write again later.   Cheerio!

Sincerely yours, Arthur

Mount Dandenong, Victoria,
23rd December, 1936.

Dear E .V.,

Thank you for remembering us and forgive me for not remembering you in time, but I have had about 100 letters from radio fans to acknowledge and to whom to send the enclosed leaflet.

The old knee is slowly but surely recovering, and I can now get about without a stick but only for short distances. Otherwise I am feeling very well and now weigh ten-five when I have not weighed over nine-seven since after Gallilpoli.

I have been thinking of you and hoping your crops were not badly damaged. Even up on this mountain the heat and humidity were bad, but what it must have been in Collins Street does not bear thinking about. Now I am in hopes of being able to get a bus next month when I can feel confident of driving it. We have been having an argument about it. I want to buy a utility and the wife wants a car as she doesn't like the idea of riding in a truck when Mrs Blank rides in a flash car. Oh, these women! So perhaps I will compromise to a degree and go in for a roomy Dodge coupe with a large dicky which could be used for storage. I saw in the paper recently where two blokes who have just rounded Australia say that all that is necessary to get over bad places is a winch. Do you know anything about these gadgets?

Yes, the squatters ought to be pleased by the rain. They had a good fall up at Wilcannia. I wish the lakes would get filled again as I would like to camp up there for week. I suppose H is still on deck - if manager hasn't shot him for boozing up. He needs only to wait six months when we shall be well mixed up in another world war, and then he will certainly be made a general or something. If he took A.G. as his batman they would make a remarkable pair.

Cheerio to both of you, and the best of a good season.

Yours ever,

Arthur

He enclosed a cutting from the *Advertiser* which printed a photograph of the author showing a lean face with a crest of thick dark hair brushed back from a broad forehead, deep-set eyes, a prominent jaw and a defensively determined expression, as if he did not expect the favourable review: Mystery in The Cattle Lands

"It may be the setting of *Wings Above the Diamantina* that has all owed Mr. Upfield to write such a gripping and unusual book. It is unusual in two ways. Firstly, it is a true mystery story, complete with an uncannily clever detective, but it is far away from fogs, tearing taxis and teeming continental crowds. Secondly, it is an Australian novel which does not recount the doings of the pioneers...

"Although early in the book the dialogue is rather unnatural, the author soon loses that awkwardness in the interest of his tale... The characters are well drawn and Mr. Upfield has the true novelist's knack of introducing small characters who have little, if any bearing on the tale, but who contribute much to the book.

"In short, an interesting and most enjoyable novel, which as a famous critic once said, 'makes one rise early in the morning'. But it is a pity that the publishers allowed a number of small typographical errors to escape their notice ."

Wings Above the Diamantina was the first of Upfield's books to be published in Australia where firms were reluctant to risk accepting any book which had not been tried overseas (see cover below). Angus and Robertson Limited had even refused the manuscripts of Katherine Susannah Prichard's *Coonardoo* and M. Barnard Eldershaw's *A House is Built*, which had shared the *Bulletin's* £1000 prize at the beginning of the thirties, however subsequent success with books of Australian history, natural history and travel written by Ion Idriess, William Hatfield[12] and other *Bulletin* contributors had encouraged further ventures.

Crime fiction sold well both in Australia and overseas and Professor Ernest Mandel in *Delightful Murder* attributes its popularity at that time to nostalgia, a longing to return to the carefree, leisurely way of life in an English country house, the location of many detective stories. Upfield broke new ground by giving that type of fiction an Australian setting.

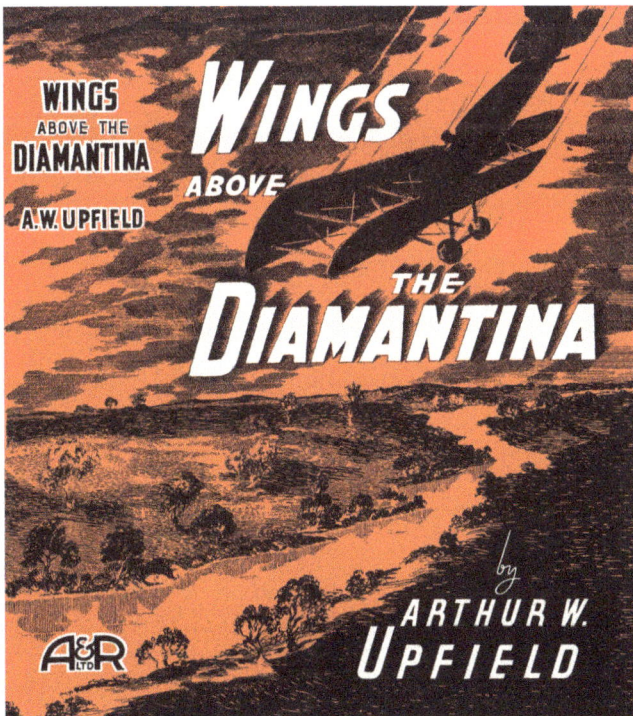

9.

SINCERELY YOURS

Mount Dandenong
Victoria. 14 June, 1938

Dear E.V.

I have never previously heard of a man getting two such knocks as you have received, and I remained awake last night thinking about it. I am myself fairly callous but I hope I will never become quite so bad as P. After Elder's letter to you in reply to yours explaining the matter and your sacrifices of fees, etc, it's worse than a bit thick. You have excellent grounds for an action; on the other hand Elders might well square matters with you with another offer in the future.

As for Mrs Whyte, well, that is a terrible misfortune but not one that cannot be mended. They do great things nowadays with that complaint and with proper care and attention she will be restored to you after a space. Your biggest problem is your children. They are safest at home with this accursed paralysis spreading. I am in no position to advise, but if I can help in any way be sure to let me know.

Things with me have been up and down. Before this warm weather came in the old leg periodically went "bung". It would be good for a week or two and then for a week or two it couldn't be bent or straightened. I fear sometimes it will never get wholly right again, and what annoys me is that it will not permit me to plan ahead.

I was writing about Syd the other night. Have been at work on my biography - three parts of it done - and after telling of Pluto and Yorky I shifted to the time I went cooking at the Lake and described how Syd and I fitted a mast to the boat, made a chaff-bag sail and sailed it across to the far side when a howling westerly blew. When half way over, Syd shouted: "There's a fence somewhere about here and there's only ten feet of water on a calm day". You know Syd's casual manner. At once I estimated that the wave troughs were at least four feet down and the top of the fence five feet up, which didn't leave much to spare between the fence tops and the bottom of the boat. We couldn't do anything. To get back was impossible, and to mess about with the sail might have broached the ship broadside on to the sea and capsized us.

The waves were travelling about our own speed. For long we rode on a crest and for long we wallowed in a trough. Then I saw a fence post top in a trough in which we were and only by a fluke did we sail between two posts and scrape on the top wire.

Since publishing with A and R I have done better but haven't made much money. During the second half of last year they sold 300 copies of *Diamantina*, proving that - as this book was published the year before - the life of a book in Australia is much longer than in England. They published *Mr Jelly's Business* last June and *Winds of Evil* last October. These are both Bony books and I am sending on a copy of each for your collection. Perhaps Mrs Whyte would like to have them.

A and R have entered into a contract on my behalf with John Hamilton Limited, London, to publish these two and *Diamantina* in English editions. Hamiltons have already published *Diamantina* under the title of "Winged Mystery", the word "Diamantina" I suppose having no meaning to English readers. Thus I save British Tax of 25% on sales in Australia, and instead of getting 3d a copy for Australian sales, as per Hutchinsons, I now get 7d a copy from Angus and Robertson. I now make about one pound per 1000 words from the volume production which is half the rate as for the short stories published in the *Australian Journal*.

However, it is long and continuous work which has a gambling chance of bringing a comparative fortune. So has a ticket in Tatts.

I have greater hopes in this autobiography[13], this kind of writing seemingly much more favourably received by the book buying public. While I have made no mention of people on Albemarle, other than Yorky - who I understand is dead - and Pluto and Moss Jones, I have given space to Wheeler's Well and Victoria Lake. There should be much to interest you...

If only a man could put into an autobiography *everything*.

Later on I'd like to have Mr Hole's address. I wrote to him once and he kindly replied with information about Sadler (sic). I owe him something for pulling me in off the track when I was down and out subsequent to my return from the war.

I've been lucky enough to get commissioned by the *Herald* to write a series of articles on the swordfishing this year, and this will enable me to go to Bermagui[14] for 10 days and land a Centenary prize - £500 for the biggest swordfish and £200 for the biggest shark caught in N.S.W.'s waters. You will be able to imagine my language if my leg should go on strike.

You know, I don't think I have written to you since my visit; which just goes to show how self-centred a bloke can be. Before retiring that night at the Wentworth pub Scribe and I had three pots of beer and we were made sick for four or five days. We reached Zanci without much trouble, and after leaving, were put on a crook track to Balranald. The track petered nearly out in whipstick mallee which damaged my bus. We finally reached a dam where the track blew right out and the Scribe wanted to come due west when I well knew that Balranald lay east of south. Anyway after scouting on foot I found the track which became rapidly better and we reached a fine station homestead not far from Box Tank on the Balranald - Ivanhoe road.

Altogether it was a fine trip.

Well now, here's knocking off hoping you get again on your feet and that Mrs Whyte's health will improve. Kindly remember me to her. Look up cheerful, or try to.

Sincerely yours

A.W.Up.

Should you see Mr Hole please mention me to him.

A.

That is the last of the letters kept by E.V. Whyte. After the writer and a companion, "Scribe" of the Australian Broadcasting Commission, had visited him and another friend of Albemarle days, Roy Vigar, then living on his property Zanci east of Pooncarie, Verco was engaged by Elder Smith Ltd. to manage a station near Menindee while its owner travelled overseas. He spent some time with him learning about the country but when he was unable to take over the management on the appointed day because of his wife's illness, the owner repudiated the contract. Those were the two knocks referred to by Arthur Upfield.

Verco's wife was suffering from tuberculosis and he took her to Kalyra Sanatorium in South Australia for treatment. Their children Pat and John stayed with kind friends in the bush, Alexander McGillivray, the manager of Lake Victoria Station west of Wentworth, and his wife. Maud Whyte recovered her health and the family was reunited at Riverview, but by that time Australia was at war once more. Both Verco Whyte and Arthur Upfield became involved in war work as well as their usual activities and had little time for letter writing.

Verco Whyte never returned to the bush to live and it was not until 1964 that he was able to make a trip around Australia, travelling with his family in a Holden car and caravan. Although a successful fruitgrower he always preferred sheep and in 1942 he bought some nearby grazing country.

Much of his time was devoted to the welfare of the Wentworth region where his organising ability, mentioned by Upfield, was soon recognised and won him the British Empire Medal for service to the community. He spent twenty-seven years in local government, becoming Mayor of Wentworth in 1949 and 1950 and serving a term as President in 1958 and '59, after the municipality had become a shire. For more than twenty years he was chairman of region four of the Murray Valley Development League. He died while addressing its meeting at Murray Bridge in South Australia on 15 June, 1972.

Arthur Upfield died at his home at Bowral on 12 February, 1964, leaving unfinished the last of at least thirty-three novels, *The Lake Frome Monster,* which was completed afterwards from the detailed notes he had left for the purpose. The setting of the story was the dog-proof fence at Quinyambie Station in the far west of New South Wales where he was boundary riding with two cunning old camels at the time he wrote his first letter to the overseer at Albemarle.

The last twenty years of his life were happy ones. In 1944 while he was still on Mount Dandenong he met a pretty, fair-haired young widow, Jessica Uren, who had come with her nine-year old son Don to Kalorama where she kept a store. The following year they went to live at Healesville, then together they built a house at Yarra Junction forty-five miles from Melbourne, naming it Atlas after the station in *Gripped by Drought.* They collaborated in writing a succession of Bony books, working as a team. Arthur was unable to find mistakes in his work once he had written it, Don Uren recalls, and he would read it aloud to her and she would correct his mistakes in spelling and any discrepancies. He was always kind to Don, giving him the care and companionship his own son had been denied during his wanderings in the bush.

Later Arthur and Jessica lived at Airey's Inlet and then on the southern coast of New South Wales at Bermagui, a popular place for fishing, Arthur's visits there in the late thirties had inspired *The Mystery of Swordfish Reef* in which Bony on the trackless sea found clues in the patterns of weather, tides and currents.

It was easier to follow a murderer over the Walls of China, a range of ancient, eroded sand dunes curving around the north-eastern rim of dry Lake Mungo, seen by the writer on his visit to his friend at Zanci. In 1948 he led an expedition sent by the Australian Geographic Society to photograph and report on a meteorite crater sixty-five miles from Hall's Creek in Western Australia and that became the scene of another crime.[15] The settings of his novels, their characters and the clues to the mysteries were all dredged from his observations of the outback and the inside country. Droughts, dust-storms, floods, the migration of rabbits, rabbit trapping, kangarooing, camels, swordfish, processional caterpillers, ants and spiders were dramatised and exaggerated to make an exciting story.

The flying spiders he described at Airey's Inlet in *The Clue of the New Shoe* were far more numerous and substantial than the whisps of white gossamer which float on a north-east wind from as far away as Queensland or even New Guinea, catching on twigs and bushes and sometimes holding minute spiderlings.

Bushmen call it "Queensland snow'" and predict rain in three days. Once at Victoria Lake on Albemarle he and Sid Whyte saw several shags stranded in a corrugated iron tank, lured there by the shining water but having no room to take off again. Sid was amused to read the description of the tank in *Death of a Lake*:

"Without difficulty he (Bony) hauled himself up to look inside, and received one of the great surprises of his life.

"It was filled almost to the brim with the carcases of cormorants… there must have been several thousand birds that had piled into this tank to die."

In the lively and interesting biography[16], *Follow My Dust*, written with Jessica Hawke (her maiden name), Arthur Upfield's memories of people and places are either dimmed by time or deliberately distorted to avoid the risk of libel. He covered his tracks so well that the record of events in the twenties and thirties is not consistent with the matter of fact account in his letters.

The years at Albemarle made an enduring impression on the writer. Aspects of his life there can be detected in many of his books and James Hole and the Whyte brothers, tall, amiable, efficient bushmen with soft voices and a wry sense of humour, were the models for his heroes. His friendship with them precluded any repetition of the cliche of the villainous boss.

The shearing team at Albermarle in the mid-1920s.

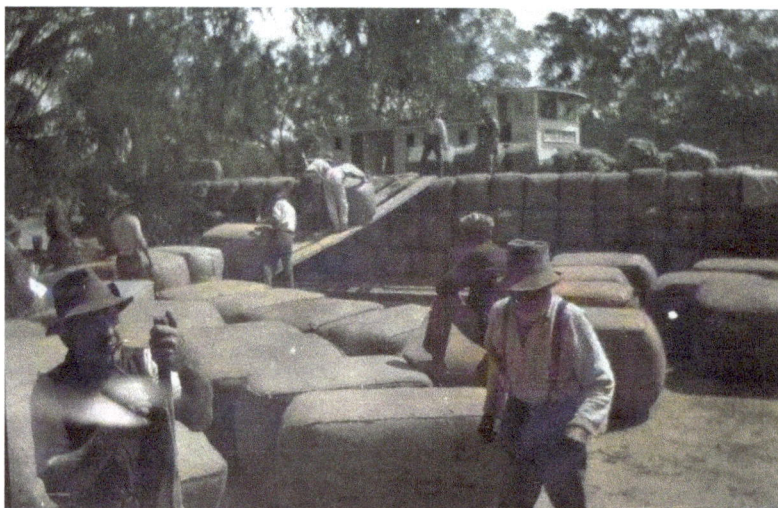

Loading Albermarle wool onto a barge to be towed by the PS *Tolarno* in 1922.

The station that he knew so well is different now. The old homestead of Albemarle[17] with its surrounding frontage country is renamed Windalle and owned by Nicholas Klemm whose family held two nearby homestead leases, one of 6,000 acres (2,428 hectares) selected from Albemarle about 1896 by Robert Rutherford and another of 5,000 acres (2,023 hectares) selected at the same time by Samuel Klemm and later combined with Rutherford's lease.

Upfield made several references in his novels to the cutting up of the large pastoral holdings for closer settlement. The Land Act of 1884, which created the Western Division of New South Wales, divided the runs into two areas, the leasehold and a resumed area to be held by an annual occupation licence until it was claimed by homestead leases. The Western Land Act of 1901 and its amending acts made further provisions, and more resumptions from Albemarle were made in 1936 and 1937 until only the outback portion remained and the outstation at Victoria Lake became the headquarters.

The eastern country was lost in 1955, leaving approximately 160,000 acres (64,752 hectares), which were divided and sold in 1964, the year of Upfield's death. The homestead block Albemarle of 80,000 acres (32,376 hectares) was bought by the manager Richard (Dick) Gloster and his wife Avril and the rest of the country by Foster Heatley, a former jackeroo and overseer. He named it Talyawalka and built a homestead beside Eucalyptus Lake for his manager David Flint, who had also been a jackeroo and overseer when Dick Gloster was managing the station.

There has been a continuity of staff as well as ownership at Albemarle. T.H.R. Broughton, who succeeded E.V. Whyte as overseer at Victoria Lake, became the manager when James Hole left in 1934, and John de Courcy Harrison, an Englishman related to the owners, was promoted to the post of overseer and then manager at the new Government House at Victoria Lake. The next manager, from March 1941 to September 1955, was W.G. Furness Martin. He was succeeded by Dick Gloster, who had been a jackeroo and overseer there from 1947 to 1951 and married Furness Martin's daughter.

Arthur Upfield did not lose touch with the friends he had made at Albemarle. Sid Whyte later had a sheep station in the lower Flinders Ranges in South Australia and his wife Patty remembers:

"I met Arthur at the train in Port Pirie when he and Jessica Hawke were travelling to Adelaide to launch *Follow My Dust*, so this must have been in 1957. Sid had received a telegram from Perth telling him that they would be passing through Pirie and asking if he might meet the train. I was always interested in his books and hearing about him."

Her cousin Isabel Currie, a daughter of James Hole, says:

"I have always understood that he began writing seriously when at Wheeler's Well on Albemarle, and that Verco, and Sid read some of his work to give an opinion. I don't think Arthur ever talked about it much. I remember him as a tall lean man who talked very quickly.

"In later years, whenever Arthur was in Melbourne, he came to see my father who had retired and come to live with me. Arthur was then living at Airey's Inlet and the two men who so loved the bush would enjoy reminiscing together. Several times my father spent a few days at Airey's Inlet with Jess and Arthur.

"I have a number of author's copies which he gave to my father. In *Death of a Lake* he has written:

For Mr James L. Hole with sincere good wishes and the hope that this tale will refresh memories of triumphs over many difficulties in the days that will never return.

Arthur Upfield's success was another triumph over difficulties, and his courage, independence and perseverence are an example to all aspiring writers. In the beginning he had no assistance except encouragement from his friends and the advice of his literary agent in England and he wrote in whatever spare time he had while earning his living in the bush. His masterstroke was the invention of his engaging Aboriginal detective, Napoleon Bonaparte.

Angus and Robertson published eight of the Bonaparte series before the beginning of World War II and after American soldiers began arriving in Australia, Bony books sold well in the United States. Bonaparte Holdings Pty. Ltd., the company which held the copyright of the books from 1956 to 2013,[18] reported that there was an incredible interest in them, especially overseas and among overseas visitors, and each year sales are increasing.

A 26-part television series - 'Boney' - was produced by Fauna Productions and aired in Australia in 1972 and '73 to popular acclaim. Every episode featured the remarkable Aboriginal dancer, David Gulpilil and James Laurenson as Upfield's detective. The series was shown in the United Kingdom, and later in Germany and France, resulting in the series in book form in both these languages.

Grundys produced a new Bony series in 1992, updated by making the hero Bony's grandson, a young white policeman who goes to a country town Woongaa to investigate the mysterious disappearance of his friend, the local police officer. The first episode was filmed in Wentworth in the autumn of 1990 but this series bore no relation to the original books or the Fauna adaptions.

A new television series is being developed by Novel Films, with episodes on the Darling River. So the restless spirit of Napoleon Bonaparte will return to the Darling River country where he was conceived ninety-five years ago.

NOTES

1. The characters mentioned in this and subsequent letters can be further clarified in the Albermarle Wages Records herein.
2. Peter Corry was a teacher at Blinman who became a well-known photographer of the region and his photographs are in the State Library of South Australia.
3. Augustus "Gus" Peirce was an American artist and actor who was in Australia in the 1870s, writing the memoir *Knocking About* (ETT Imprint). He navigated the Murray and spent many years as captain of steamers in the Murray-Darling area.
4. Coonardoo was a novel written by Katharine Susannah Prichard (Mrs Hugh Throssell) published in 1929.
5. The "heir" was John Verco Whyte, born in 1928.
6. Bony as a character in Upfield's novels was based on Upfield meeting with tracker Leon Wood.
7. E.V. Whyte's wrote paragraphs for the *Bulletin* under the name "Bush-Cat", at the same time as Ion Idriess was writing as "Gouger" and Upfield was being rejected.
8. Published as *The Great Melbourne Cup Mystery* (ETT Imprint, 1995)
9. *Breakaway House* (ETT Imprint, 2016)
10. Upfield wrote 13 stories for *Walkabout* magazine and these have been collected in book form as *Walkabout* (ETT Imprint, 2021)
11. This biography was published as *The Gifts of Frank Cobbold* (ETT Imprint, 2016)

12. Ion Idriess served at Gallipoli with the Australian Light Horse, all the way to Beersheba. He published over 50 books. Arthur Upfield served in the same places as a lorry driver. Upfield died in 1964, Idriess in 1979 and William Hatfield, author of *Sheepmates* (1931) died in 1969

13. Upfield's autobiography was not published in his lifetime. It was finally published as *Beyond the Mirage* (ETT Imprint, 2020)

14. For more details and photographs of Upfield's time at Bermagui, we refer you to *Bony at Bermagui* (ETT Imprint, 2021)

15. Hall's Gap is the setting for *The Mountains Have a Secret*.

16. *Follow My Dust* (ETT Imprint, 2017)

17. For a full historical perspective on the ownership of Albermarle, we refer you to *Big Men Long Shadows: A Story of the History and Happenings of a Sheep Station on the River Darling, 'Windalle'* by Claudia Richards-Mousley (2010)

18. In 1956 Angus & Robertson encouraged both Upfield and Idriess to move their copyrights into a family-based company - thus Bonaparte Holdings for Upfield and Idriess Enterprises for Idriess. In 2013 Bonaparte Holdings reversed this decision, putting all of Upfield's intellectual property in the hands of Upfield's grandson, William Upfield.

The Rabbit Department,
Burracoppin, W.A.,
4th August 1930.

Dear E.V.,

Very many thanks for your letter of July 21st. I am very glad to receive your opinion of Atonement, and sorry to hear that it received the knock.

An example of Upfield's handwriting (see page 61), courtesy of William Upfield.

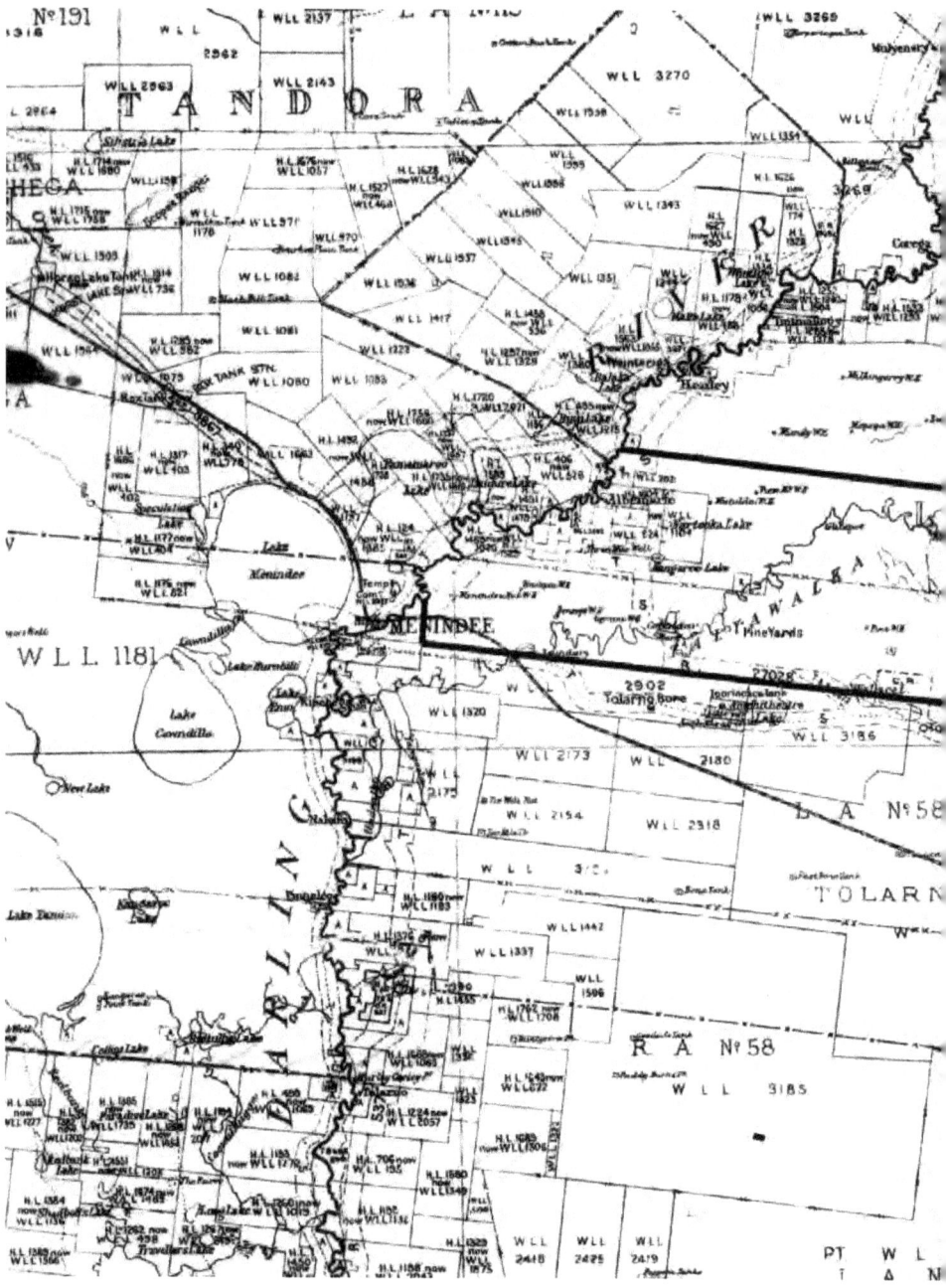

MAP OF ALBERMARLE STATION IN 1928. Courtesy of Alan Whyte.

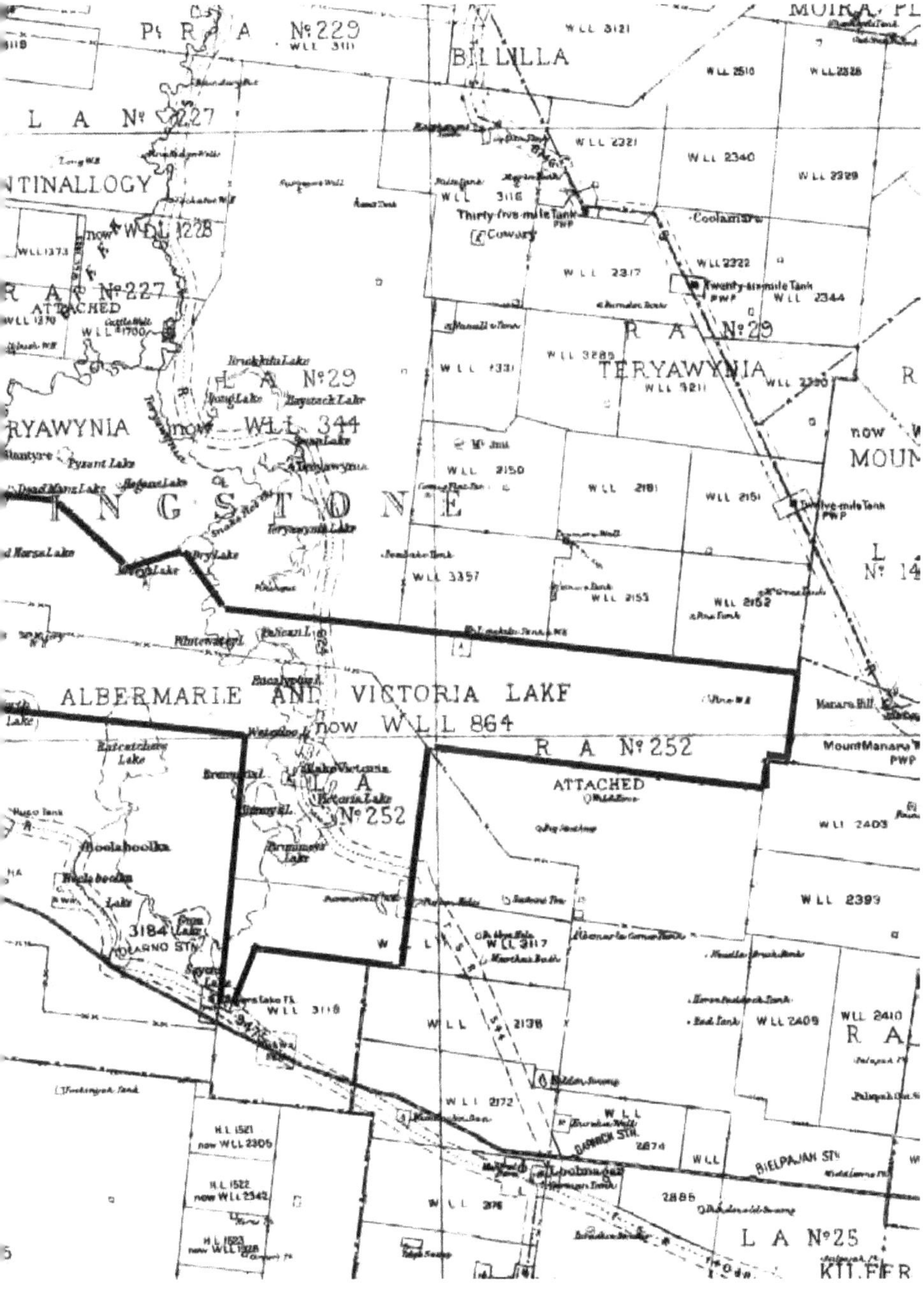

BILLILLA
WLL 2340
TINALLOGY
Thirty-five-mile Tank
Coolamara
WLL 2317
WLL 2322
Twenty-six-mile Tank
WLL 2344
R A No 29
TERYAWYNIA
L A No 29
RYAWYNIA
WLL 2150
WLL 2181
WLL 2151
NGSTONE
Twelve-mile Tank
WLL 3357
WLL 2155
WLL 2152
ALBERMARIE AND VICTORIA LAKE
now WLL 864
R A No 252
ATTACHED
Mount Manara
WLL 2403
WLL 2399
Boolaboolka
WLL 3117
WLL 2409
WLL 2410
WLL 2138
WLL 2172
WLL 2874
BIELPAJAH STN
GARNICK STN
2885
L A No 25

Bony Novels by Arthur Upfield
published by ETT Imprint:

1 The Barrakee Mystery / The Lure of the Bush

2 The Sands of Windee

3 Wings Above the Diamantina

4 Mr Jelly's Business/ Murder Down Under

5 Winds of Evil

6 The Bone is Pointed

7 The Mystery of Swordfish Reef

8 Bushranger of the Skies / No Footprints in the Bush

9 Death of a Swagman

10 The Devil's Steps

11 An Author Bites the Dust

12 The Mountains Have a Secret

13 The Widows of Broome

14 The Bachelors of Broken Hill

15 The New Shoe

16 Venom House

17 Murder Must Wait

18 Death of a Lake

19 Cake in the Hat Box / Sinister Stones

20 The Battling Prophet

21 Man of Two Tribes

22 Bony Buys a Woman / The Bushman Who Came Back

23 Bony and the Mouse / Journey to the Hangman

24 Bony and the Black Virgin / The Torn Branch

25 Bony and the Kelly Gang / Valley of Smugglers

26 Bony and the White Savage

27 The Will of the Tribe

28 Madman's Bend /The Body at Madman's Bend

29 The Lake Frome Monster

Other Titles by Arthur W. Upfield published by ETT Imprint:

1 The House of Cain

2 The Beach of Atonement

3 A Royal Abduction

4 Gripped by Drought

5 Breakaway House

6 The Murchison Murders

7 The Gifts of Frank Cobbold

8 The Great Melbourne Cup Mystery

9 Follow My Dust

10 Up & Down Australia

11 Up & Down the Real Australia

12 Up & Down Australia Again

13 Beyond the Mirage

14 Walkabout

15 Bony at Bermagui

Upfield's own drawing of Bony

www.ingramcontent.com/pod-product-compliance
Lightning Source LLC
Chambersburg PA
CBHW051209090426
42740CB00021B/3436